Pregnancy & birth

The essential checklists

Pregnancy & birth

The essential checklists

Canadian Edition

Karen Sullivan

DK

Project Editor Angela Baynham
Designer Hannah Moore
Senior Editor Helen Murray
Canadian Editor Barbara Campbell
Senior Art Editor Liz Sephton
Picture Librarian Romaine Werblow
Production Editor Kelly Salih
Senior Production Editor Jenny Woodcock
Production Controller Mandy Inness
Creative Technical Support Sonia Charbonnier
Managing Editor Penny Warren
Managing Art Editor Glenda Fisher
Category Publisher Peggy Vance

First Canadian Edition, 2009

Dorling Kindersley is represented in Canada by
Tourmaline Editions Inc.
662 King Street West, Suite 304
Toronto, Ontario M5V 1M7

09 01 11 12 13 10 9 8 7 6 5 4 3 2 1

175541—October 2009

Published in Great Britain by Dorling Kindersley Limited.

Library and Archives Canada Cataloguing in Publication

Sullivan, Karen
Pregnancy & birth : the essential checklist / Karen Sullivan. --
Canadian ed.
Includes index.
ISBN 978-1-55363-114-9
1. Pregnancy--Popular works. 2. Childbirth--Popular works. I.Title.
II. Title: Pregnancy and birth.

RG525.S88 2009 618.2 C2009-902654-6

Printed and bound in China by Hung Hing Printing Group Ltd

Discover more at
www.dk.com

Contents

Introduction

Whether having a baby is part of your long-term plans or an unexpected surprise, becoming pregnant is an emotionally charged, life-changing event. And as the hormones begin to surge through your body, you find yourself faced with the daunting task of juggling pregnancy and work, planning the birth, and preparing for your new life with a baby. There is a bewildering array of choices to think about and arrangements to be made, not to mention coming to grips with the idea of becoming a mom.

But help is at hand. This indispensable little book will ease you through the process of organizing your life and help you sail through pregnancy, plan the birth you want, and deal with day-to-day life with your newborn. You'll find tips for everything from common health issues, arranging and decorating your baby's nursery, and purchasing essential equipment, to planning your birth and choosing the best birth options and pain relief, selecting the right childbirth classes, planning for childcare, coping with pregnancy and new motherhood while at work, and bathing your new baby and encouraging her to sleep.

We'll look at how to stretch your budget to accommodate your new arrival, your rights and benefits during pregnancy, and what to expect from your healthcare providers at every stage. You'll find logs for charting your baby's sleep and feeding patterns and her growth and development, and vital information to ensure that your baby is happy, healthy, and stimulated. We'll look at travel and transportation, packing the perfect hospital bag, keeping your handbag equipped with pregnancy essentials, and what your baby needs in her diaper bag. I'll also provide you with an at-a-glance list of symptoms that confirm you are in labor, and a handy checklist for your birth partner, too.

Once your baby is here, I'll talk you through the early days of feeding, dealing with everything from breastfeeding problems and support to preparing those first bottles and even weaning. I'll lead you through the immunization schedule, common health issues and teething, and the processes of registering your baby's birth and arranging for her first passport. I'll also help you choose the perfect toys and games to keep your baby contented and entertained at each stage during her first year.

Whether you are a first-time mom-to-be or a seasoned expert, this book will be very useful. Its handy checklist format allows you to see at a glance what exactly is needed in any circumstance or situation, which allows you to use your precious time wisely, checking off the essentials as you move through the months to stay on top of what needs to be planned and purchased. What's more, there is space allowed at the end of every checklist for you to add your own ideas and details, making each list even more relevant and personal to you and your baby.

Pregnancy & Birth: The Essential Checklists will not only help you to stay on top of things, but it will keep you one step ahead, leaving you with all the time you need for the things that really matter.

Karen Sullivan

Pregnancy

What to do if the test is positive

The confirmation that you are about to become a mother heralds a new stage in your life, and now is the perfect time to start planning and preparing for the changes ahead. You may be experiencing mixed feelings about the news, and that's entirely normal. Beginning the preparations can help you to come to terms with your new status.

- ○ **Take a second test**—although modern pregnancy tests are very accurate, they can sometimes be wrong
- ○ **Make an appointment to see your healthcare provider** (ob/gyn, family physician or registered midwife) who will book you in (see page 12); see page 73 for tips on choosing a midwife
- ○ **Let your doctor know if your immunizations are not up to date**
- ○ **Avoid taking new medications**, and consult your doctor if you need to take any regular medication
- ○ **Calculate your estimated delivery date** (see box, opposite)
- ○ **If you aren't already taking folic acid, start now**, since this is essential for your new baby's development
- ○ **Cut out alcohol and cigarettes**, which have been linked to health problems in babies
- ○ **Develop a healthy eating plan** (see pages 18–19), with plenty of fresh fruits and vegetables, lean protein, good-quality carbs, and foods rich in iron and folic acid
- ○ **Exercise moderately**—staying in shape helps to ensure an easier pregnancy and birth (see pages 28–29)
- ○ **If you usually drink coffee, cut back** or try decaffeinated coffee or tea instead; a little caffeine won't hurt your baby, but caffeine has been linked to miscarriage in some women
- ○ **Listen to your body**—if you are tired, take a nap; if you are hungry, have a snack; the very best way to overcome and cope with the symptoms of pregnancy is to listen and respond to your body's signals
- ○ **Share the news**—some women like to wait until they've had an ultrasound or passed the 12-week mark, but there's no reason why you can't tell a few people your good news now

○ **Make sure you have a good support network** of friends, family, and your partner, as well as your doctor and/or midwife, who can answer the multitude of questions that are likely to crop up during the coming months

○ **Join an online community of pregnant women** and new moms who can share advice and stories

○ **Start a pregnancy diary**, writing down how you are feeling, what symptoms you are experiencing, and any hopes or plans you have for the months to come; ask your partner or a friend to take a photo of you every month to keep track of your changing body

○ **Invest in a few pregnancy books** to keep tabs on what's happening to your baby—and you!

○ **Look around for good prenatal classes**—although you are unlikely to begin these for several months, they may get booked up well in advance

○ **Sign up for weekly pregnancy updates via email**—these are based on your estimated due date; good ones to try include pregnancy.about.com and www.babycenter.ca

○ **Enjoy your pregnancy**

○ ....

○ ....

○ ....

Your estimated due date

This date is calculated by adding seven days to the first day of your last menstrual period, and then subtracting three months. So, if your last period was on February 1, your baby will arrive somewhere around November 8. Some experts believe that caucasian first-time moms should add an extra 15 days to this date; however, your first scan will pinpoint an accurate date.

Prenatal appointments and tests

Once your pregnancy is confirmed, you will be regularly monitored to ensure that both you and your baby are healthy and well. Different testing methods are used in different parts of Canada—talk to your caregiver about your specific situation.

Routine prenatal appointments (with your midwife or physician)

Most pregnant women have between 10 and 15 routine prenatal appointments, and you will need to set up these visits. You can expect to see your healthcare provider at approximately:

- ○ **8 weeks** (doctors, obstetricians and midwives like to see you by 8 weeks now, so that the first dating scan is likely to be more accurate)
- ○ **10–12 weeks** (booking-in appointment)
- ○ **16 weeks**
- ○ **20 weeks**
- ○ **24 weeks**
- ○ **28 weeks**
- ○ **30 weeks**
- ○ **32 weeks**
- ○ **34 weeks**
- ○ **36 weeks**
- ○ **37 weeks**
- ○ **38 weeks**
- ○ **39 weeks**
- ○ **40 weeks**
- ○ **41 weeks** (assuming you haven't had your baby)

These dates will differ between regions and doctors or midwives.

Blood tests

A small sample of your blood will be tested for:

- ○ **Your blood group and a Complete Blood Count (CBC)**, which screens for problems such as anemia
- ○ **Your rhesus status** (whether you have a positive or negative blood group)
- ○ **HIV** (optional but recommended)
- ○ **Hepatitis B**
- ○ **Syphilis**
- ○ **Rubella immunity**
- ○ **Toxoplasmosis**
- ○ **Genetic tests** (depending on your ethnic background and medical history)

Ultrasound scans

Most women have one or two ultrasound scans, although you may be offered more if you have a high-risk pregnancy. You may also be scanned later to check the size and position of your baby or placenta. Otherwise, expect scans at:

- ○ **10–13 weeks**—this "dating scan" is routine for some practitioners; they'll also check for multiple babies or an ectopic or molar pregnancy
- ○ **11–14 weeks**—Nuchal Translucency (NT) scan to check for chromosomal abnormalities, such as Down's syndrome, and congenital heart problems; some areas do not offer the specialist equipment required for this scan
- ○ **18–20 weeks**—to confirm dates, check your baby's heartbeat, confirm your baby's location, measure your baby, detect twins, check location of the placenta, assess the amount of amniotic fluid, check for physical abnormalities, and try to determine your baby's sex

Screening and diagnostic tests

- ○ **Blood tests** in early and mid pregnancy to check for chemicals indicating abnormalities, as well as high glucose levels that could suggest gestational diabetes; at 35–37 weeks you may be checked for Group B Streptococci
- ○ **Urine is tested** at each appointment to check for protein (a sign of pre-eclampsia), urinary tract infections, and sugar (a sign of diabetes)
- ○ **Blood pressure** is checked at every appointment to ensure its stability

If screening tests suggest that your baby has a high risk of Down's syndrome or other chromosomal abnormalities, you may be offered:

- ○ **Chorionic villus sampling (CVS)**, in which tiny samples of the chorionic villi (finger-like projections on the placenta) are taken to check the genetic information they carry:
  - ○ transvaginal CVS is done at 11–13 weeks, when a small tube or forceps are inserted through your cervix
  - ○ transabdominal CVS is usually done after 13 weeks, when a needle is inserted through your abdomen into your placenta
- ○ **Amniocentesis**, in which a needle is inserted into your womb, and amniotic fluid is removed for testing; this is done after 14 weeks, and usually offered to women over the age of 40

- ○ ....
- ○ ....

Budgeting for baby

Early pregnancy is a great time to look closely at your financial situation and plan ahead. There's no doubt that having a baby can be expensive, but with a little tweaking of the budget, and some prudent cuts, you can help to make sure that you are in a comfortably stable financial position to enjoy life as a parent.

- ○ **Figure out how much you spend each month** (include all regular events)
- ○ **Consider swapping service providers for better deals**
- ○ **Consider paying utility bills online**, or arrange for automatic payment by credit card or automatic withdrawal to avoid late fees
- ○ **Check your bank statements** to be sure that regular transfers and direct debits are correct, up to date, and necessary
- ○ **Take a look at your credit card spending**; it might be a good idea to consolidate credit card debt on the card with the lowest interest rate; once you've paid off the balance, pay your bill in full every month
- ○ **Plan out income and expenditure** based on income you will be receiving while you are on maternity leave
- ○ **Plan as though you have less income than you expect**, which will give you some flexibility if you decide to go back to work a little later than planned, or if you decide to work fewer hours on your return
- ○ **Make sure you are getting all the benefits** to which you are entitled
- ○ **Take into consideration any shortfalls in your medical insurance**, or the cost of having your baby at home or hiring a doula or midwife
- ○ **Childcare may be your single greatest cost** when raising your baby; check with your provincial or territorial government to see if you qualify for a childcare subsidy
- ○ **Consider your car**: you are going to need something practical, reliable, and big enough to fit child safety seats and carry baby gear—if you have a sedan, you may want to consider changing to a station wagon, SUV, or crossover vehicle
- ○ **Start putting some money aside each month** to use after your baby is born; even a few dollars a month will accumulate

- ◯ **Add up the estimated costs of "running" your baby**—include childcare, babysitting, diapers, formula (if you don't intend to breastfeed), baby equipment and clothes, baby toiletries, and toys and books
- ◯ **Buy one key item for your baby each month**, to spread out the cost
- ◯ **Register big items**, such as your baby's crib, stroller, and car seat, on a "wish list" at a good department store or baby superstore. so that friends and family looking for gifts can get you what you really need (see page 78)
- ◯ **Remember that the most expensive items** are not necessarily the best
- ◯ **Don't be proud**! Ask family and friends with older children to lend you secondhand equipment or clothes, and visit yard sales or eBay
- ◯ ....
- ◯ ....
- ◯ ....

Your basic maternity wardrobe

While pregnancy is a great opportunity to purchase a new wardrobe, it's wise to cut corners where you can. For one thing, your maternity clothes may never be worn again after the birth of your child. Here are some great ideas for dressing well—and on a budget.

- **Think about the seasons for which you are shopping**, so you don't end up with a collection of long-sleeved maternity tops if you'll be heavily pregnant in summer
- **Start with a few items and add pieces as you need them**—aim to buy one or two new items every month throughout pregnancy to keep reviving your maternity wardrobe
- **For the office, purchase a few pieces** of neutral, simply shaped basic garments, and accessorize them with scarves and jewelry
- **Don't hesitate to accept offers of maternity clothes** from friends and relatives; wearing these clothes at home will leave you with a little more money to spend on clothes for going out
- **Keep your own style and comfort level in mind**—if you weren't comfortable wearing dresses or sweater sets before your pregnancy, you are unlikely to be so now
- **Buy quality, feel-good clothes**—you are going to be wearing these a lot
- **Invest in two good-quality maternity bras**, and don't be surprised if they need to be replaced in a few months
- **Maternity underwear is an unnecessary expense**—just buy a larger size; however, this doesn't apply to other maternity clothing, which is specially designed to accommodate your growing bump
- **It's worth investing in a good pair of maternity pants**—something stretchy, with an adjustable waist, or low-slung trousers that can sit neatly under your growing bump
- **If you've got an old pair of jeans** that are ready for recycling, cut out the front, and sew in an elasticized panel
- **Raid your partner's cupboard**—large T-shirts or dress shirts can be pulled in with a low-slung belt to create comfortable maternity wear that doesn't impact on your budget
- **Empire-cut dresses** will see you through most of your pregnancy

- **You can purchase a "belly band,"** which is designed to fill the gap between shirts or tops and pants, as your waist expands
- **Don't forget your shoes**—your center of gravity changes when you are pregnant as your weight shifts forward, and high heels can be dangerous (not to mention uncomfortable); look for elegant flats or shoes with a low heel
- **In the summer**, opt for clothing made of natural fabrics, such as linen and cotton; loose-cut dresses and pants and flowing skirts and tops will help you stay cool
- **Think twice before investing in a winter coat**—you are likely to feel very warm toward the end of your pregnancy, and may find it more comfortable to wear plenty of layered knits rather than one coat or jacket
- ______________________________
- ______________________________
- ______________________________
- ______________________________

Nutrition during pregnancy

By now you'll be aware that what you eat is very important during pregnancy. A healthy diet not only helps ensure that your baby gets all the nutrients he needs for optimum growth and development, but it also minimizes the risk of pregnancy complications, and provides you with plenty of energy. Your healthy pregnancy diet should include:

- **Whole grains**, such as whole-wheat bread and pasta, brown rice, legumes, and grains (such as barley, oats, and quinoa), to provide a sustained source of energy, plenty of fiber (see opposite), and essential B vitamins
- **Good sources of calcium**, to ensure the healthy development of your baby's bones and teeth—you'll find calcium in dairy products, soybean products, leafy green vegetables, and some fish
- **Folic acid**, for your baby's nervous system; look for it in dark green vegetables, nuts, and whole grains
- **Protein**, which is necessary for the development of every new cell in your baby's body—good-quality protein is found in legumes, whole grains, nuts, soybeans, dairy, eggs, lean meats, poultry, and fish
- **Vitamin C**, which not only helps your body to fight infection and maximizes the absorption of iron, but is also essential for the growth of a strong placenta—fresh fruit and vegetables provide plenty of iron

- ○ **Iron-rich foods**, which help to prevent anemia, and ensure that your baby builds up adequate iron stores; try lean red meats, leafy green vegetables, fish, dried fruits, beets, wholegrain bread, and iron-fortified cereals
- ○ **Fiber**, to ensure that nutrients are efficiently absorbed, and your bowel movements are regular—whole grains should give you plenty
- ○ **Essential fatty acids**, which are necessary for your baby's development, particularly his nervous system, brain, and vision—good sources include eggs, nuts, seeds, and cold-water oily fish (such as salmon and mackerel)
- ○ **Fresh water**, to keep you and your baby well hydrated
- ○ ....
- ○ ....
- ○ ....

Foods to avoid during pregnancy

- ○ **Liver and cod liver oil**—these can provide too much of the animal form of vitamin A, which is linked to birth defects
- ○ **Meat pâtés**, which can contain food-borne illnesses
- ○ **Unpasteurized soft or blue cheese**, such as Camembert, goat's cheese, Brie, and Stilton—these can contain listeria
- ○ **Raw or partially cooked eggs**, as these can contain salmonella
- ○ **Raw or undercooked meat, fish, and poultry**—these can contain salmonella or *Toxoplasma gondii*, which can cause toxoplasmosis
- ○ **Ready-to-eat salads in bags** (without thoroughly washing) because of the risk of listeria
- ○ **Shark, swordfish, king mackerel, and tilefish**, which contain high levels of mercury; limit other fish and shellfish to two servings a week
- ○ ....
- ○ ....
- ○ ....

Perfect pregnancy snacks

Not only does your blood sugar have a tendency to dip and soar during pregnancy, leaving you feeling tired and lethargic, but your body needs regular refueling to keep up with the demands placed upon it. Treat your snacks as "mini meals": they should be balanced and contain plenty of essential nutrients (see pages 18–19), with no empty calories.

Great snack ideas include:

- ○ **Nuts or seeds**
- ○ **Plain live yogurt with fresh fruit**
- ○ **Fresh fruit and vegetables with dips**
- ○ **Toast with nut butters or high-fruit spreads**
- ○ **Fruit smoothies**
- ○ **Vegetable soup**
- ○ **Dried fruit**
- ○ **Good-quality, low-sugar granola bars**
- ○ **Cheese sticks**
- ○ **Small sandwiches with plenty of salad**
- ○ **Pasta or couscous salads, with lots of veggies**
- ○ **Whole-grain, unsweetened breakfast cereal**
- ○ **Hard-boiled eggs**
- ○ ....
- ○ ....

Bedtime snacks

Have a snack before bed to help you sleep and to ensure you don't wake up with hunger pains. Go for turkey, eggs, and dairy produce, all great sources of the amino acid tryptophan, which encourages restful sleep.

Your pregnancy handbag

It's a good idea to stock your handbag with everything you need to deal with pregnancy symptoms and the daily reality of being pregnant on the go. Useful items include:

- ○ **Sanitary napkins**, for spotting or leaking
- ○ **A plastic or lined paper bag**, in case you are sick
- ○ **A travel toothbrush**, to freshen up after sickness
- ○ **A small spray bottle of water**, for when you experience flushes
- ○ **Bottled water** to keep you and your baby hydrated
- ○ **Cream or lotion** for dry skin or itching
- ○ **Wet wipes** for freshening up
- ○ **Your doctor's phone numbers**
- ○ **Details of an emergency contact**, in the event that you become unwell and help is required
- ○ **Ginger candy** for nausea
- ○ **Sunscreen**, to help prevent melasma
- ○ **Healthy snacks** to keep blood-sugar levels steady
- ○ **A suitable antacid**
- ○ ....
- ○ ....
- ○ ....

When to take extra care

If you carry an extra pair of shoes in your pregnancy handbag, make sure you wrap them in a plastic bag to prevent the spread of microorganisms picked up from the ground. Always rinse out your water bottle before refilling it to prevent bacterial growth, and get rid of any used tissues, which can harbor germs.

Maternity rights and benefits

There are very strict guidelines supporting your rights during pregnancy. At present, maternity (and parental) leave is different according to the province or territory you live in. It's always a good idea to investigate what's on offer, so that you know where you stand—and talk to your employer about any additional maternity benefits that they may offer.

Maternity leave and pay

- **During your leave**, the federal government pays you benefits through the Employment Insurance Act (EI), which replace a portion of your salary; benefits are not available to self-employed individuals
- **You are eligible** for these federal EI benefits if you've worked a minimum of 600 hours of ensured work in the last 52 weeks or since your last claim
- **The basic rate** for all EI benefits is 55 percent of your average insured earnings, up to a maximum payment of $447 per week; the maximum payment period is 15 weeks for maternity benefits, and 35 weeks for parental benefits
- **Maternity EI benefits** are paid exclusively to biological mothers
- **Parental EI benefits** can be paid to either one of the biological or adoptive parents, or split between them in whatever proportion they choose; if a mother chooses to take both her maternal and the complete parental benefits together, she could receive a total of 50 weeks' benefits
- **Pregnant employees** have the right to take Pregnancy Leave, which is unpaid time off work, provided they meet certain criteria; employers do not have to pay wages to someone on Pregnancy Leave, but some will; each province and territory sets a time limit for Pregnancy Leave
- **New parents** have the right to take Parental Leave, which is unpaid time off work when your baby is born; leave can be taken by either parent or shared between them, and ranges from 35–37 weeks
- **Check with your employer** about using your accumulated sick leave, vacation, and personal days for maternity leave
- **Short-term disability insurance** can be purchased to cover a portion of your salary when you are unable to work due to illness, injury, or childbirth

- **Residents of Quebec** are covered by the Quebec Parental Insurance Plan (QPIP)—to be eligible, Quebec residents need only have earned $2,000 in insurable income during the reference period and pay QPIP premiums

Enhanced maternity leave

- **Your employer may offer its own package**, which may involve a longer period of maternity leave (paid or unpaid), and a higher percentage of your income paid for the period that you are receiving federal benefits; they may also pay an additional portion of your salary during your leave

Rights

- **During the time that provincial law protects your job**, your employer cannot lay you off, fire you or penalize you in any way because you take maternity or parental leave
- **While you are on leave**, you still accumulate seniority as you did while you were working; you can also continue to participate in employee pension plans, as well as life and health insurance plans, unless you ask not to
- **When you return from leave**, you employer is required to reinstate you in your current position, or its equivalent, with the same benefits
- **Pregnancy is a valid health reason** to be away from work (for prenatal appointments or tests for example)—check with your company to see if this time will be paid for, or if you need to use sick or vacation days
- ______
- ______

Prenatal time off

You must inform your employer in writing that you wish to take a pregnancy or parental leave. Your notice should include the date you plan to start your leave and the date you plan to return to work. You must give at least four weeks' notice.

Your pregnancy-at-work toolkit

Being prepared to deal with any pregnancy symptoms during working hours can help you to feel on the ball and remain professional with a minimum amount of fuss. You may want to include:

- ○ **Bottles of fresh water** to stay hydrated and alert
- ○ **Decaf coffee or tea**
- ○ **Healthy snacks** to keep you going (see page 20)
- ○ **Natural remedies** for headaches, heartburn, and nausea (see pages 36–37)
- ○ **A cushion, heating pad, or hot water bottle** for backache
- ○ **A footstool to keep your feet up** (under your desk, of course)
- ○ **An alarm clock**, in case you manage to catch a few winks during a break
- ○ **A toothbrush and toothpaste**, to help recover from vomiting episodes
- ○ **A notebook** listing ongoing projects and their status
- ○ **Your job description**, highlighting your regular routines and tasks
- ○ **A list of everyone you work with** and their contact details
- ○ **A master list of file names and locations** on your computer, with a password set up to access all personal files
- ○ ....
- ○ ....
- ○ ....

Rest and recharge

Take extra breaks now and then to recharge your batteries if you need to, but make sure you keep up with your work and maintain a professional manner to set the standard for how people treat you and your pregnancy.

Hazards at work

It is completely safe to continue working in most jobs while pregnant. However, it is important to be aware of any potential risks to you and/or your baby. If your job involves any of the situations listed below, you are within your legal rights to ask for changes to be made to your job description and working practice.

- ○ **Working with animals**, which may carry *E. coli* or organisms that cause tularemia, toxoplasmosis, or histoplasmosis
- ○ **Working with chemicals**, such as those used in medical, dental, or pharmaceutical occupations, as well as in painting, cleaning, farming, dry-cleaning, gardening, pest-control, and carpet-cleaning
- ○ **Exposure to food hazards**, such as listeria, *E. coli*, and salmonella, which can be encountered by handling raw foods
- ○ **Exposure to secondhand smoke**, which crosses the placental barrier and increases the level of carbon monoxide in your baby's developing brain
- ○ **Exposure to radiation**, from X-rays
- ○ **Exposure to viral hazards**, in medical settings or even childcare facilities, where you may be in contact with viruses that may harm your baby
- ○ **Requirement to do heavy lifting**
- ○ **Long hours spent standing or sitting**
- ○ **Working excessive hours**
- ○ **Working in awkward spaces and work stations**
- ○ **Working under stress**, an excess of which has now been linked to low birth weight, high blood pressure, and possible developmental and behavior problems in your baby
- ○ **Exposure to violence**
- ○ **Wearing a tight-fitting uniform**, which can make you uncomfortable and exacerbate pregnancy symptoms
- ○ ....
- ○ ....
- ○ ....

Traveling during pregnancy

Unless you fall into the high-risk pregnancy category, it's perfectly possible to travel safely during pregnancy, as long as you take sensible precautions and ensure that you are prepared for the unexpected.

- ○ **Before planning your trip**, consult your doctor to discuss any potential risks particular to your pregnancy
- ○ **Avoid traveling to parts of the world** where there is a high risk of disease
- ○ **Avoid live vaccines**, such as chicken pox, measles, mumps, and rubella, since these are usually not recommended in pregnancy
- ○ **Remember that oral vaccines** to protect against yellow fever, typhoid, polio, and anthrax are contraindicated during pregnancy
- ○ **Tetanus, hepatitis, and flu shots** are considered to be safe, but discuss with your doctor
- ○ **Take with you any regular medication or remedies**—you may not be able to find what you need at your destination, or you may be delayed
- ○ **Check with your airline in advance**: some won't allow you to fly past 36 weeks without a current doctor's letter confirming your due date and fitness to fly
- ○ **Check with individual travel-insurance companies** to be sure that pregnancy is covered
- ○ **Arrange for an aisle or bulkhead seat** for extra leg room
- ○ **Wear your seat belt under your belly** and across your lap
- ○ **Reduce the risk of deep-vein thrombosis**, which is more likely during pregnancy, by drinking plenty of fluids, remaining as mobile as you can, and wearing support stockings while flying
- ○ **In developing countries**, only eat fruit you have peeled yourself; avoid leafy greens and salads, which may have been washed in contaminated water
- ○ **Drink bottled water**
- ○ **Travel light** and make sure you can easily pull or carry your luggage
- ○ ....
- ○ ....
- ○ ....

Dealing with sleep problems

Feeling exhausted throughout pregnancy is absolutely normal, but the weight of your baby can make it difficult to sleep, and common pregnancy symptoms often occur at night. However, help is at hand.

- ○ **Get regular exercise**, which encourages healthy, restful sleep
- ○ **Eat tryptophan-rich foods** before bed (see page 20)
- ○ **Have a warm (not hot) bath** about 30 minutes before bedtime, and add 8–10 drops of lavender oil (check with an aromatherapist first)
- ○ **If you suffer from restless legs**, increase your intake of folic acid (see page 18), and, when RLS strikes, immerse your feet in a bucket of cold water, then return to bed with your feet raised on a pillow
- ○ **Avoid caffeine and other stimulants**, which discourage sleep
- ○ **Try a cup of warm milk** to relax and encourage sleep
- ○ **Don't watch TV in bed** if you're having trouble sleeping; experts recommend that you should only use your bed for sleep and sex
- ○ **Keep your clock out of sight** if seeing the time will make you anxious
- ○ **Use cushions and pillows** to support your growing bump while you sleep
- ○ **Ask your partner for a massage** to help reduce tension
- ○ ....
- ○ ....
- ○ ....

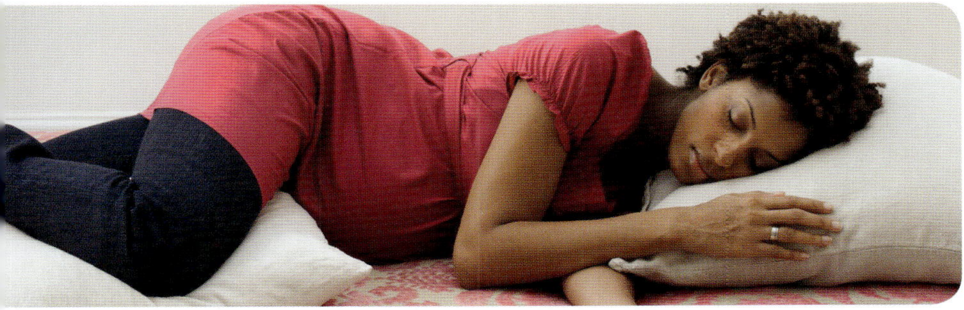

Ideal exercise

Even if you've had a sedentary lifestyle until now, you can safely start an exercise program during pregnancy—just check with your doctor before you get going. Not only will exercise help you maintain a healthy weight, but it will also promote restful sleep, encourage circulation and elimination, reduce tension, and get your feel-good endorphins flowing.

- **Don't exercise to lose weight** or suddenly "shape up"; instead, exercise at a mild to moderate level
- **Start slowly and build up**: 15–20 minutes at a time, three days a week, is plenty for beginners
- **Never exercise past the point at which you can no longer talk**
- **Swimming** will help keep you fit and supple without putting pressure on your joints
- **Yoga** eases tension, and encourages flexibility and strength

- ◯ **Walking**—even gentle—is an easy way to stay fit and experience the benefits of exercise
- ◯ **Running and jogging** are fine, if you've done them before—make sure you have good shoes, and don't push yourself too hard; this is great training for chasing your toddler-to-be
- ◯ **Cycling** supports your weight, but you can be at risk of falling as your center of gravity shifts; instead, try a stationary bike, and start slowly
- ◯ **Stair-climbing machines** will raise your heart rate and keep you fit; hold on to the side rails for support
- ◯ **Aerobics or aquarobics** classes are fine, but choose one for pregnant women that has been adapted for safety and health
- ◯ **Dancing** is very good exercise, and can get your heart pumping; avoid spinning or jumping, though, which may cause a fall
- ◯ **Pelvic floor exercises** (Kegel exercises) are not only recommended, but essential; strengthening these muscles can help you through labor and delivery, and minimize bladder leaks and hemorrhoids
- ◯ **Always keep yourself well hydrated**, stopping for sips of water as you go
- ◯ ....
- ◯ ....
- ◯ ....

What not to do

Some activities should definitely be avoided, including high-risk sports, horseback riding, downhill skiing, snowboarding, waterskiing, and scuba diving. Avoid ab exercises that have you lying flat on your back. Weight-lifting and other exercises that involve standing in one place for longer periods can decrease the flow of blood to your baby. The best advice? Keep moving!

Coping with pregnancy symptoms

Some women sail through pregnancy without any symptoms at all, while others suffer from every possible ailment. The good news is that whatever your complaint, there are ways to cope. However, if you are at all worried, talk to your doctor.

Easing morning sickness

- **Symptoms are often worse when you are hungry**, so eat little and often to stabilize your blood-sugar levels
- **Drink plenty of water**—dehydration can make nausea worse
- **Eat a little first thing in the morning** before you get out of bed
- **Avoid fatty foods and junk foods**, which seem to make symptoms worse
- **Ginger is a traditional remedy for morning sickness**; you can drink ginger tea or ginger ale, or chew crystalized or candied ginger until symptoms pass
- **Take vitamin B6 regularly**, since deficiency appears to be a factor
- **Invest in a motion-sickness wristband**; strap it onto your wrist so the plastic button presses against an acupressure point on your inside wrist —some research suggests this can help ease nausea and vomiting
- **Get plenty of sleep** and take regular rests—this can make a big difference in the way you feel
- **Try to remember that almost all cases of morning sickness pass** by the end of the first trimester, when your hormones settle down
- **Dry cookies or crackers** seem to help ease nausea for many women

It's safe to feel sick

There is evidence to suggest that women who experience severe nausea are less likely to miscarry; morning sickness is believed to be caused by high levels of pregnancy hormones, which help to keep the pregnancy safe.

Coping with constipation

- **Make sure you drink plenty of water**, which helps to keep things moving in your bowels
- **Fiber is crucially important**—aim for five or six servings of fruit and vegetables a day, preferably with skins, and boost your intake of whole grains (see page 18)
- **If you need a little help**, psyllium or ispaghula husk (*Plantago ovata*) are effective unblockers, and safe during pregnancy
- **Keep up the exercise**, which will help to keep you regular
- **Try a little reflexology** (see page 36): massage the base of the heel of your foot, and the arch, pushing your thumb down evenly and deeply; several studies have found that this really works
- **Massage your abdomen** with a teaspoon of slightly warmed olive oil—this will help to stimulate bowel movements
- **Ask your doctor** if he can adjust your iron-supplement dosage, if need be; iron can cause constipation

Reducing swelling and edema

- **Exercise regularly**—this helps to encourage healthy circulation, and disperse fluid buildup
- **Drink plenty of fresh water**—this is, without doubt, the best natural diuretic around
- **Put your feet up regularly** to take the pressure off your circulatory system and direct the blood and fluid to your baby
- **Reduce your salt intake**, and make sure you are getting enough protein, both of which can discourage fluid retention
- **Include lots of natural diuretics** in your pregnancy diet, such as asparagus, pumpkin, onions, grapes, beets, parsley, green beans, pineapple, and garlic
- **B vitamins**, found in good levels in whole grains in particular, can act as a natural, mild diuretic
- **A good massage** can reduce fluid buildup and encourage healthy circulation

Relieving heartburn

- **Eat little and often**, to avoid overfilling your tummy
- **Eat a slice of fresh pineapple** (not canned) after every meal; the digestive enzymes it contains work wonders to prevent acid buildup
- **Avoid lying down right after meals**, which can cause acid to enter the upper digestive tract
- **Avoid citrus fruits**, or, if you do eat them, make sure you do so along with a little protein, to discourage acid buildup
- **Coffee, tea, and carbonated drinks** will make matters worse, so skip them
- **Elevate the head of your bed** by 4–6 inches (10–15 cm) to lower your risk of heartburn while lying down
- **Avoid fatty and fried foods**, which take longer to digest, giving more time for acid to swish around your digestive system
- **Slippery elm powder** mixed with water or milk will protect the mucus membranes lining your digestive system, and ease symptoms
- **Sad but true**: chocolate can cause heartburn!
- **If all else fails, take an antacid after meals**, or as required—choose calcium carbonate, which is generally considered safe in pregnancy
- **Remember that heartburn usually ceases the moment you give birth**

Handling headaches

- **Eat and sleep enough**—deficits during pregnancy can cause headaches
- **Get a little exercise**, which encourages the pain-killing hormones, endorphins, and improves circulation
- **Drink plenty of water**—many headaches are caused by dehydration
- **Apply a cold compress** at the base of your neck
- **Eat fresh, whole foods** to prevent headaches caused by blood-sugar swings
- **If you experience** blurring of vision, vomiting, bright lights, or a headache that simply won't go away, see your doctor immediately

Beating back pain

- **Shift your position** as often as you can, to avoid putting strain on any one part of your body
- **Put a footstool** (or even a pile of books) under your feet to reduce the pressure on your back when sitting
- **When lying down**, raise your feet with some pillows
- **Try relaxation exercises**, such as clenching and relaxing every part of your body in order, from head to toe
- **Yoga and other stretching exercise** will help loosen areas of tension
- **Exercise encourages circulation**, which disperses areas of congestion that cause pain; it also encourages the "feel-good" hormones to flow
- **Bend at the knees** when lifting heavy objects such as groceries or toddlers
- **Don't sit or stand** for long periods without a break
- **Try placing an ice pack on your back for a few minutes**, several times a day, to reduce inflammation
- ....
- ....
- ....

When to see your doctor

If pregnancy symptoms fail to ease, or if they become debilitating, it is important to get them checked out. As a precaution, always see your doctor if you experience any of the following:

- ○ **A negative pregnancy test that follows a positive one**—this could indicate hormone problems or ectopic pregnancy
- ○ **Anxiety or confusion**, perhaps with a racing heart or rapid breathing
- ○ **Heavy bleeding** or passing clots of pink, grey, or red material
- ○ **Painful cramping**, particularly if accompanied by bleeding
- ○ **Any illness that lasts longer than 48 hours**, such as vomiting, diarrhea, and even colds or flu
- ○ **A high temperature**
- ○ **Extreme headaches**
- ○ **The baby stops moving**
- ○ **Sudden swelling of your face or hands**
- ○ **Vision problems**
- ○ **A sudden loss of pregnancy symptoms**, such as morning sickness
- ○ **Severe abdominal pain** and tenderness
- ○ **Pain during urination**
- ○ **Difficulty breathing or chest pain**
- ○ **Extremely itchy skin** that won't respond to soothing creams
- ○ ....
- ○ ....

When to act

As your pregnancy progresses, you will become more attuned to your body and more familiar with the aches, pains, and other discomforts. However, if you experience sudden, extreme symptoms of any nature, call your doctor.

What to ask your doctor

Many women feel embarrassed about bombarding their doctors with questions, but rest assured that they will always be happy to answer even the most obvious queries, and to take the time to reassure you. Here are some ideas to help you get to the bottom of things.

- ○ **Is everything going OK** with my pregnancy?
- ○ **What can I do to help my baby grow healthily** and stay well myself?
- ○ **Are my symptoms normal?**
- ○ **What types of medications are safe** during pregnancy?
- ○ **I've had some spotting**—will my baby be OK?
- ○ **What do the results of my tests and screening mean?**
- ○ **Is it safe to have a massage during pregnancy?**
- ○ **Is it OK to dye my hair during pregnancy?**
- ○ **Which prenatal classes would you recommend?**
- ○ **How can I monitor my baby's heartbeat?**
- ○ **Where can I have my baby?**
- ○ **Can I have a home birth or water birth?**
- ○ **What can I do to get labor going?**
- ○ **How can I tell the difference between real contractions and Braxton Hicks?**
- ○ **Who should I call when I go into labor?**
- ○ **What happens if my doctor isn't available when I go into labor?**
- ○ **How long should I stay at home** before I go to the hospital?
- ○ **Will I have the same nurses** for my entire labor?
- ○ **Can I say "no" to interventions during labor,** and if so, which ones?
- ○ **Can I have an elective Caesarean section?**
- ○ **Where can I find a lactation consultant?**
- ○ ....
- ○ ....

Natural therapies and remedies

Many women are understandably reluctant to take conventional medication during pregnancy. There are some alternative and complementary therapies and remedies that are safe during pregnancy, but talk to your doctor before starting something new. Always make sure the practitioner knows you are pregnant.

The best natural therapies

- **Reflexology**: applies pressure to reflexes on hands or feet to encourage relaxation, increase circulation, and stimulate healing; it can help with pain relief during labor, and a host of pregnancy-related symptoms
- **Acupuncture**: uses small, thin needles to balance energy in the body, which runs through pathways known as meridians; plenty of research shows that it is effective in a wide range of pregnancy symptoms, can help with the pain of childbirth, and can even help turn a breech baby; regular treatment encourages overall good health and wellbeing—for both you and your baby
- **Flower essences**: diluted extracts of various flowers and plants are used to balance negative emotions that can be the cause of illness; excellent for tension, shock, anxiety, fear, depression, exhaustion, and even coping with change
- **Chiropractic**: hands-on manipulative therapies that can ease any symptoms with a structural root, such as back pain, headaches, circulation problems, and even heartburn
- **Massage**: the perfect therapy for pregnancy—it encourages healthy circulation and the removal of waste products, relaxes and restores, helps to disperse edema, and eases tension
- **Aromatherapy**: uses essential oils to balance your body and mind; it can help ease a number of pregnancy symptoms. Many experts frown on aromatherapy during pregnancy; the effects of most plant oils on pregnant women is unknown, and some may be hazardous during pregnancy

- **Homeopathy**: uses heavily diluted substances that work on your body's energy field to encourage healing on all levels. Speak with your doctor before using any homeopathic products; homeopathy has been the subject of scientific controversy. If your doctor gives you the go-ahead, visit a certified homeopath to see if he can provide treatment

The best natural remedies

- **Raspberry leaf tea** is believed by some to shorten labor—it has been associated with increased uterine contractions, but very little research has been done on pregnant women using raspberry-leaf products, so unless your doctor says it's OK, it's best to avoid these until your pregnancy is full-term
- **The herb yellow dock** is rich in iron, and an excellent way to address anemia—drink as a tea or in tincture form
- **Witch hazel and/or lemon juice** can be applied neat to hemorrhoids (piles), to reduce swelling and bleeding; sitz baths in hot water two to three times a day can also be soothing
- **Massage your big toe firmly to ease headaches**—this is a useful DIY reflexology trick
- ....
- ....
- ....

Complementary caution

Complementary therapies can be extremely useful during pregnancy, but only at the hands of a registered, experienced practitioner. "Natural" doesn't always mean "safe," so make sure you know what you are taking and why.

Stimulating your baby

Whether you simply want to spark your baby into reassuring action, change her into a more comfortable position, or start encouraging her to respond to you, there is plenty that you can do to get your baby to move around and to keep her stimulated.

- ○ **Stop and relax**—if you are up and busy all day, your baby will be lulled to sleep by the regular movement
- ○ **Lie down on your side with your bump supported**; this position seems to stimulate your baby to move to accommodate your new position
- ○ **Drink a sweet, icy-cold drink**—this should nudge her into action
- ○ **Talk to your baby**—by the fifth month her hearing is developed and she will hear and respond to your voice
- ○ **Encourage dad to get up close and talk to your baby**—getting to know the voices of mom and dad will come naturally, but she'll be likely to hear much more of mom's, and will be intrigued by dad's voice up-close
- ○ **Read stories or poems aloud**—most children's books have rhythmic and rhyming words, helping your baby understand the ebb and flow of language
- ○ **Singing songs**, such as lullabies, can soothe your baby
- ○ **Music is proven to stimulate babies**, and evidence suggests that a daily dose of Mozart may stimulate your baby's brain and senses; play loud music—this not only wakens her but also stimulates her to move
- ○ **Feel free to play games**—push her little foot or elbow when she moves it outward, and watch her shift her position; do it over and over again
- ○ **Watch the effect of a strong light held against your womb**: your baby will respond to the light; this is a good trick to try if you need to keep baby awake during the day to prevent nightly gymnastics sessions
- ○ ....
- ○ ....
- ○ ....

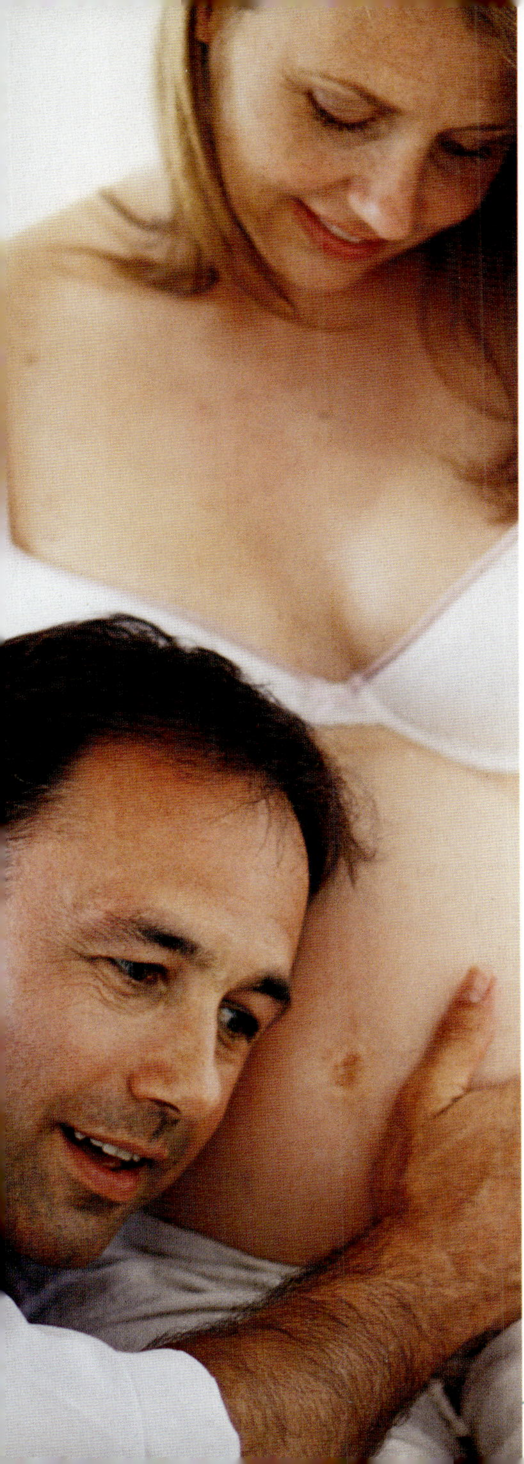

Simple stimulation

Your baby can be stimulated through all sorts of external experiences; in fact, studies have shown that by the 24th week her heart rate increases in response to stroking or patting your abdomen.

Preparing for baby

Essential first clothes

Although you are likely to receive plenty of clothes for your new baby from well-wishers, it makes sense to have the basics ready before birth. Try to restrain yourself, though—babies outgrow their clothes very quickly. If you want to invest in an expensive outfit or two, buy them in bigger sizes so that he will get more wear from them.

- ○ **Babies are messy**—you'll need several items in each category of clothing to ensure you aren't chained to the washing machine, or always waiting for something to dry
- ○ **Choose uncomplicated outfits** that will open easily for quick (and middle-of-the-night) changes
- ○ **Opt for soft, comfortable clothing** that is machine washable and doesn't have fussy (or itchy) seams or tags
- ○ **Remember that your baby will spend the majority of his first weeks sleeping**, so cozy pajamas and onesies are your best bet

Aim for:

- ○ **1–2 nightgowns**—even if your baby is a boy; these are fantastic in the early days for easy changing
- ○ **5–8 one-piece pajamas**—choose loose-fitting, soft all-in-ones, with snaps, rather than buttons or zippers that can be fiddly and uncomfortable
- ○ **5–8 undershirts**—short-sleeved are fine, even in winter, and act as an extra layer to insulate your baby; choose cotton, and preferably all-in-ones, which snap shut at the bottom, preventing uncomfortable shifting
- ○ **1–2 sweaters or jackets**—go for light options, which can be layered, and avoid anything that has to be pulled over your baby's head
- ○ **5–8 pairs of socks or booties**—if your little one is wearing footed pajamas, he won't necessarily need these, but you may want to keep his toes warm if he's trying out some other pieces in his new wardrobe
- ○ **1 warm coat or snowsuit**—choose a style with a detachable hood, if possible, and an easy zipper fastening

Color coordinates

When shopping for baby outfits, make sure you choose clothes in complementary colors so individual items can be easily mixed and matched. If you need to make a quick change, you won't have to replace the whole ensemble.

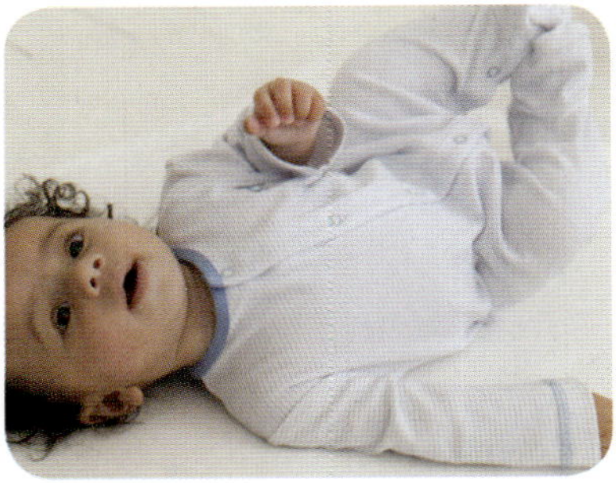

- ○ **1–2 hats**—choose one with a wide brim for summer, or something soft that covers the ears for winter
- ○ **4–5 bibs**—although your baby isn't actually "eating" yet, he'll undoubtedly create some mess with feedings
- ○ ....
- ○ ....
- ○ ....

Which diapers?

Choosing diapers can be something of a minefield. The good news is that there are now plenty of options, and you can make informed choices that are right for you and your family.

- **Whatever you choose**, remember that babies go through 10 or more diapers a day in the early weeks, and you'll need to be prepared
- **Don't buy too many of the same size**—babies grow very quickly
- **Some parents mix and match**, choosing to use disposables while out and about and/or at night, and cloth diapers the rest of the time

Cloth diapers

Pros

- **Your baby will be wearing soft, natural fibers** next to her skin
- **They come in a range of colors and styles**
- **Velcro-closing reusable diapers are now available**
- **Despite the larger initial investment**, they are cheaper in the long run
- **Cloth diapers produce less waste**, and use fewer raw materials

Cons

- **Washing produces a lot of waste water**, and uses cleansing agents and chemicals; however, on balance, reusables do less environmental damage than disposables
- **Washing can be time-consuming**
- **They take time to air-dry**, and using a tumble dryer undermines their environmental advantage
- **Your baby will need to be changed more often**, as reusables tend to be less absorbent
- **You will need to purchase accessories** such as liners and covers
- **You will have to carry wet and soiled diapers home** when you are out

Disposable diapers

Pros

- ○ **They are more convenient**
- ○ **They do not require any additional accessories**
- ○ **They are super-absorbent**, so fewer changes are required
- ○ **They cause fewer cases of diaper rash**
- ○ **They often fit better**, with fewer leaks
- ○ **Biodegradable versions made from natural materials** are now available

Cons

- ○ **They are much more expensive**
- ○ **They require proper disposal**
- ○ **They produce high levels of waste**, causing a negative environmental impact
- ○ **They usually contain manmade chemicals**
- ○ ______________________________
- ○ ______________________________
- ○ ______________________________

Bathtime essentials

It's easy to get carried away and think you need a truckload of supplies to get your tiny baby fresh and clean; however, you probably need to buy much less than you think.

- ◯ **Baby bath**—choose a sturdy plastic model that will not bend and spill its contents when moved; fill using a hose attachment to avoid having to lift the bath in and out of the tub; some models are specifically designed to fit into your kitchen sink, which keeps you from having to bend over a tub —however, after a few months, your baby will certainly outgrow this model
- ◯ **A kitchen or bathroom sink** lined with an old sheet (for comfort) is also effective as a baby bath and is better for your back; or you can bring your baby into the bath or shower with you—just be sure that you have a secure grip on him, because he'll be more slippery when wet
- ◯ **2 towels**, preferably hooded to keep your baby's head warm while you use the body of the towel to dry him; you need two because babies often empty their bladders or bowels after a bath, and you may have to start over
- ◯ **Baby bath and shampoo**—a combined product can save both money and time; organic baby products are less likely to contain chemicals that could harm your baby or cause irritation to his tender skin
- ◯ **A sponge**—natural is best
- ◯ **A cotton washcloth**—choose one with a pattern to distract your baby for times when baths are not popular
- ◯ **A plastic cup or small bucket**—this makes it much easier to rinse hair, and can also be used as a distraction
- ◯ **A non-slip mat**—this is useful if you are bathing your baby in the big tub
- ◯ **A thermometer**—not essential, but if you are concerned with getting the water temperature just right, this can come in handy; otherwise, use your elbow to ensure that water is just warm to the touch
- ◯ ....
- ◯ ....
- ◯ ....

Keeping clean

It's astonishing how much mess a small baby can create, and it can help to be prepared with a few useful items to protect his clothing and keep him clean between baths.

- ○ **Burp cloths**—these are invaluable, so invest in a whole stack: you can use them to mop up spit up, milk, and drool, and they can be used to protect your clothes when you feed and burp your baby
- ○ **Bibs**—these will protect your baby's clothes during (and shortly after) feeding, and also prevent spilled milk from irritating the skin around his neck; if he's a real drooler, he can wear them all day
    - ○ Choose bibs that are washable, and preferably ones with a wide neck that slip easily over his head; ties and snaps may prove the undoing of you if you have only one hand free
    - ○ You may wish to purchase disposable bibs for when you are traveling, or away from home
    - ○ Bibs with a cloth front and waterproof backing are particularly good, since they prevent liquid from being absorbed into your baby's clothes
- ○ **A plastic-backed mat**—for playtime, as well as feeding. If, like most babies, yours has a tendency to explosive elimination, you'll most definitely want to invest in one of these; disposable mats are also available
- ○ **Keep a supply of thin washcloths**—these can be dampened and used to clean all of your baby's little crevices
- ○ **Cotton balls**—keep these near the changing table—they can be useful for mopping little noses and eyes
- ○ **Wipes**—you'll need these wherever you are, in or out of the house, so stock up; go for natural, organic wipes, which are less likely to irritate your baby's skin
- ○ ____________________
- ○ ____________________
- ○ ____________________

Soothers and comfort items

You may want to think ahead about whether you want to use soothers such as comfort toys, blankets, and pacifiers. These can provide an easy, way to soothe an anxious or sleepless baby, and may even help to reduce separation anxiety as your baby gets older. Below are some things to take into account.

Pacifiers

- **These are particularly effective**, since they allow your child to suckle —an instinctive and calming activity
- **Some research suggests** that babies who go to sleep with pacifiers have a reduced risk of SIDS
- **Prolonged use of pacifiers** and thumb-sucking for long periods can affect your baby's speech development and the alignment of her teeth, so limit their use
- **Choose "orthodontic" pacifiers**, which are designed to have less impact on your baby's growing teeth
- **Experiment with a few brands and shapes** to see what your baby likes best, and make sure you choose the size appropriate to her age
- **When you find a pacifier that works**, buy several, and keep them in a plastic bag to keep them clean
- **Remember that pacifiers** need to be washed regularly, and should be discarded if they show cracks or tears

Comfort items

- **Choose a washable soft toy or blanket** and always use it to settle your little one to sleep, and to comfort her when she is distressed—it will soon become something she uses to soothe herself when you are not around
- **Studies have found that comfort objects help children adapt better** to stressful situations (such as beginning day care or moving to a new house), and cope better when they are anxious or afraid

- **When your baby becomes attached to a particular item**, purchase at least one duplicate immediately—this can be used while the original is in the wash, or in the event that you lose or misplace the original
- **To help make an item more attractive to your baby**, you can wear it under your shirt for a few hours so it picks up your scent
- **Comfort items become wonderful transitional objects** when your baby is separated from you (see page 185)
- **If you aren't comfortable** having your baby become attached to an object, read her the same story or sing her the same song when you are settling her—this will soon become familiar and therefore a useful tool for soothing
- ______________________________
- ______________________________
- ______________________________

Transporting your baby

There are literally hundreds of products on the market for getting your baby from A to B, and some of them are extortionately expensive. Try to remember that almost everything your baby needs for getting around will need to be replaced in a few short months, as he outgrows them. So go for functional and safe, rather than top of the line.

Car seats

- **You may wish to consider a travel system**, which allows you to transfer your baby from car to stroller/carriage base without removing him from his seat—if so, your car seat will be part of the package
- **Choose a car seat with an easy-to-fasten belt**; some are fiddlier than others, and can cause enormous frustration when you are in a hurry or your baby is distressed—you want to be able to get him in or out fast
- **Look for seats with a removable, washable cover**
- **Babies up to about 22 lb (10 kg)**—or between 0 and 9 months—will need a rear-facing seat; in fact, Transport Canada recommends that you keep your baby in a rear-facing seat for as long as possible
- **Some car seats are designed only for the first six or nine months**, others can be adapted to face forward and carry babies up to about 29 lb (13 kg). These infant-toddler seats may last longer, but experts recommend going for an infant seat first, as it is contoured to hold and protect your baby
- **Ensure that your car seat meets the Canada Motor Vehicle Safety Standards** (CMVSS); seats bought in Europe or the US may not be appropriate
- **Choose a seat with a five-point harness, for safety**
- **You must use a tether strap to anchor a seat that becomes forward-facing** when your baby gets a little older; some seats are designed to be both rear- and forward-facing. If your car does not have a tether anchor in place, contact a dealership to have one installed
- **Experts recommend that you do not use a second-hand car seat**—however, if it has all of its original parts and labels, fits your car, has never been in a crash, and is not past its expiration date, it should be OK. Note that products that are more than six years old are outdated, and likely too run down to be considered safe

Strollers

- ○ **Specialty strollers**, such as joggers and foldable, umbrella types, are popular—but the latter is really only appropriate for short trips, and definitely only after the age of six months
- ○ **Look for a carriage-style stroller** that converts to an upright stroller when your baby is old enough to sit
- ○ **Look for a stroller that can face toward you as well as outward**; your baby can see your face when she's small, and you can access her easily
- ○ **Make sure it fits in the family car when folded**, and is light enough to carry
- ○ **Choose a stroller that is easy to fold**—holding a baby in one arm and trying to collapse a stroller with the other can be tricky
- ○ **Consider the terrain you'll be treading**—if you are a country mom, you may need something that can cope with rougher surfaces
- ○ **Make sure your stroller is designed to fit through standard doorways**
- ○ **Test-drive your stroller before you buy**
- ○ **Good suspension and large wheels** will give baby a more comfortable ride

Slings

- ○ **Slings keep your hands free**, so you can keep baby close while doing chores at home, or go out without a big piece of equipment
- ○ **Make sure your partner comes along** to try out the sling
- ○ **If you plan to have several wearers**, choose a wrap-style carrier—this style is usually one-size-fits-all
- ○ **To protect your back and shoulders**, look for wide straps and padding
- ○ **Chest slings are better for new babies**; you can graduate to one that fits on your back when your baby is a little older
- ○ **Look for brands and styles that open easily for changing**
- ○ **Look for a sling that will allow your baby to face in or out**
- ○ ....
- ○ ....

Breast- and bottle-feeding

It goes without saying that you are unlikely to need much more than a comfortable place to sit if you are breastfeeding; however, you may find there are a few items that make the process easier. Bottle-feeders need very specific equipment, which must be kept clean at all times.

Breastfeeding equipment

- ○ **3–4 good-quality nursing bras**, professionally fitted, if possible; fastenings should be easy to open with one hand
- ○ **Breast pads** to deal with leaking breasts
- ○ **Breast shells** (optional) to catch drips and keep your nipples dry
- ○ **A breast shield**, for sore nipples
- ○ **Nipple cream** to relieve sore, cracked nipples—choose one that does not contain peanut oil, which is linked with allergies in children, and that can be ingested safely by your baby; organic is best
- ○ **A special nursing pillow** to make the experience more comfortable

If you plan to express, you'll also need:

- ○ **A pump** (hand-held electric, battery-operated, or manual); electric pumps can often be rented
- ○ **2–4 feeding bottles** to store your expressed milk
- ○ **Nipples** (see opposite)
- ○ **A dishwasher and/or brush** to clean the pump, bottles, and nipples
- ○ **Specialized plastic bags** or bottles for freezing your milk

Expression technique

Most women find it easier to express milk in a quiet, relaxing place. Others find they need to be near their babies for the let-down reflex to kick in. You could try expressing from one breast, while feeding your baby from the other—although this may require supreme juggling skills and manual dexterity.

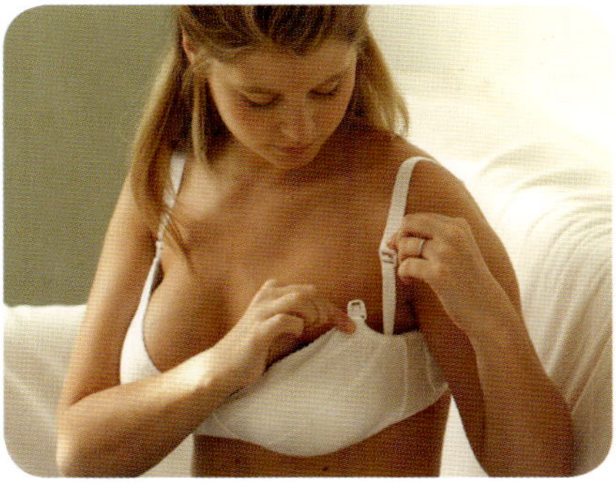

Breast- and bottle-feeding

Bottle-feeding equipment

- ○ **6–8 bottles**—smaller bottles are more suitable for newborns and babies who do not consume much milk at a sitting; you can progress to bigger bottles as your baby grows and requires larger quantities
- ○ **6–8 caps and nipples**—these should be slow-flowing for new babies; silicone nipples are more durable, whereas latex ones are closer to the feeling of a real breast—choose from a traditional bell shape or an "orthodontic" nipple, which manufacturers claim resembles a breast
- ○ **Sterilizing equipment**—choose from steaming, boiling, using sterilization solution, or microwaving; you can also sterilize bottles in a dishwasher that reaches at least 176°F (80°C)
- ○ **A nylon bottle brush**
- ○ **A tea kettle**—you'll need a regular source of boiled water available, sometimes almost instantly
- ○ **A designated measuring scoop, spoon, and knife**
- ○ ....
- ○ ....
- ○ ....

Bottle choices

There are a variety of different bottles available, including anti-colic and disposable bottles, and a choice between glass and plastic; investigate the options and choose the one that is best for your baby and your lifestyle.

Your baby's nursery

This is where the fun starts! Although the expense of furnishing a nursery can be daunting, most parents enjoy the process of decorating. There are plenty of ways to get the baby equipment you need on a budget, and also lots of things to bear in mind to ensure that the décor is safe for your new baby.

Nursery equipment

- **A Moses basket, crib, or bassinet** (optional)—many babies sleep better in small confines in the early days, but these are soon outgrown
- **A full-sized crib, with a new mattress** (see opposite)—you may wish to use receiving blankets to swaddle your baby, to make her feel cozier. You can also purchase a crib divider that attaches to the crib with Velcro tabs
- **Bedding**: 3 mattress protectors, 3 fitted sheets, 3 top sheets, 2–3 blankets (duvets are not suitable for very young babies as they tend to be too heavy and pose a risk of suffocation); layering blankets can help to keep your baby at the right temperature; Health Canada recommends against the use of bumper pads as they pose a risk of suffocation or strangulation
- **Changing area**—a purpose-built changing table is not essential; any hard surface at hip height will work, including the top of your baby's dresser or your baby's crib; the safest place to change your baby is on the floor
- **Changing mat**—go for one that is easily washed
- **Baby monitor**
- **Basic toiletries**
- **Newborn diapers** (see pages 44–45)
- **Mobile** over the baby's crib
- **Music box** to play soothing tunes
- **Soft rug** or mat made of natural fibers, for tummy time and playtime
- **Bouncy seat**, which can be moved from room to room
- **Night light**
- **Black-out shade** to ensure your baby's sleep is not disturbed by sunlight
- **Diaper pail**—preferably with a tight-fitting lid

Decorating

- ○ **Choose a low- or zero-VOC** (volatile organic compound) paint, which does not contain the unhealthy chemicals contained in traditional paints; or go for natural paints made from water, clay, chalk, plant dyes, and beeswax
- ○ **Opt for hardwood flooring** paired with a rug made of natural fibers, or choose a low-VOC carpet, and clean with a HEPA-filtered vacuum cleaner —carpets harbor dust mites, dirt, and allergens, and emit VOCs into the air
- ○ **Choose all-wood furniture** with non-toxic finishes; furniture made from particle boards or veneers can release gases such as formaldehyde
- ○ **Make sure there are no strings, electrical sockets, or electrical cords** near your baby
- ○ **Give the ceiling some consideration**: if there is something stenciled or painted on, or hanging from the ceiling, it will fascinate your baby

Your baby's crib

- ○ **Choose a frame with a non-toxic finish**, such as beeswax
- ○ **A crib with adjustable height** will ensure that your baby can use it until she is ready to move into a bed
- ○ **Choose a drop-side crib**, which will allow lifting access without placing undue strain on your back
- ○ **If purchasing secondhand**, make sure the crib was made after 1986 to ensure that it meets safety standards
- ○ **Even if your crib is secondhand, buy a new mattress**—look for one with all-organic cotton filling or wool casings, and avoid mattresses that contain the fire-retardant polybrominated diphenyl ethers (PBDEs)
- ○ **Bedding should be washable**, and preferably 100 percent organic cotton; it should never contain flame-retardant PBDEs
- ○ **Teething rails can help prevent damage** to the crib when your baby starts to look for things to chew on
- ○ ....
- ○ ....
- ○ ....

Your baby's medicine cabinet

Putting together a well-stocked medicine cabinet will ensure that you are ready when illness or discomfort strike. Keep everything together in one place, well out of reach of little fingers. You won't need all these items right away, but it's good to be prepared.

- ○ **Diaper rash cream**—rashes are inevitable for babies; diaper creams containing zinc oxide are best for soothing irritated skin and providing a barrier
- ○ **Petroleum jelly**—this is useful for dry skin, diaper rash, and eczema, and provides a good barrier; if you prefer to avoid petroleum products, look for a natural balm that contains beeswax
- ○ **Teething gel**
- ○ **Baby acetaminophen**, which is good for fevers and pain relief—it's usually only appropriate after two months of age; always read the label
- ○ **A rehydration solution**—use this on the advice of your healthcare professional in the event of diarrhea or vomiting
- ○ **Antibacterial cream** for cuts and scrapes
- ○ **Baby-safe sunscreen**—preferably organic

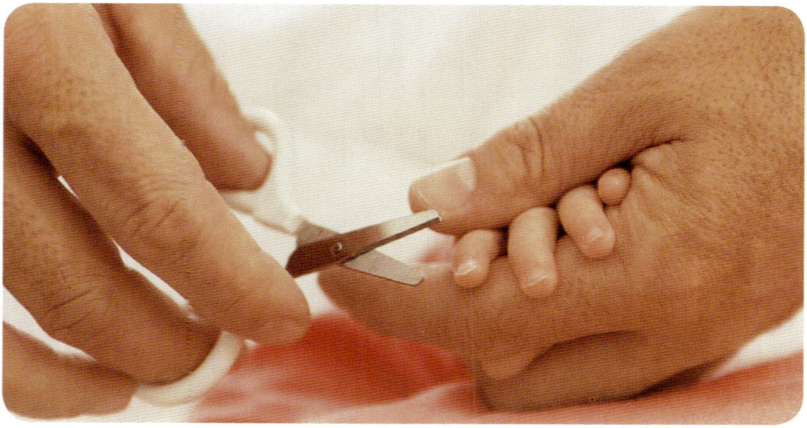

- ◯ **Medicine syringe or dropper**, to ensure that your baby gets the right dosage, and you can squirt it in gently
- ◯ **Nail clippers or scissors**
- ◯ **A thermometer**—there are a number of varieties available (see page 113)
- ◯ **Cotton swabs** to clean the folds of the outer ear (never put these inside the inner ear canal)
- ◯ **Cotton balls** to clean the eyes and wipe away any buildup on the neck folds
- ◯ **Band-Aids and adhesive bandages** in both baby and child sizes
- ◯ **A good first-aid manual** specialized for the treatment of babies and children
- ◯ ....
- ◯ ....
- ◯ ....
- ◯ ....
- ◯ ....

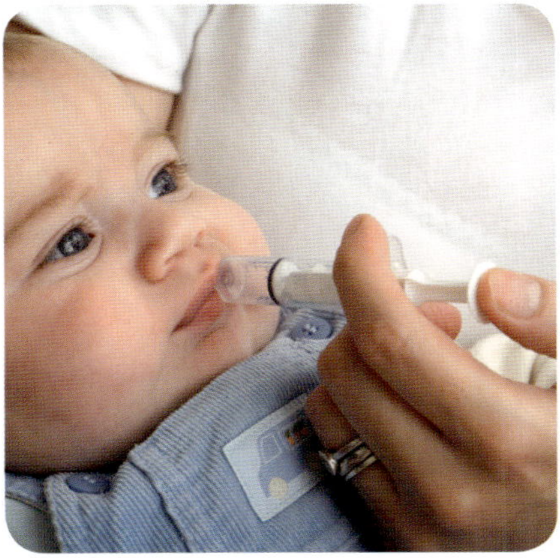

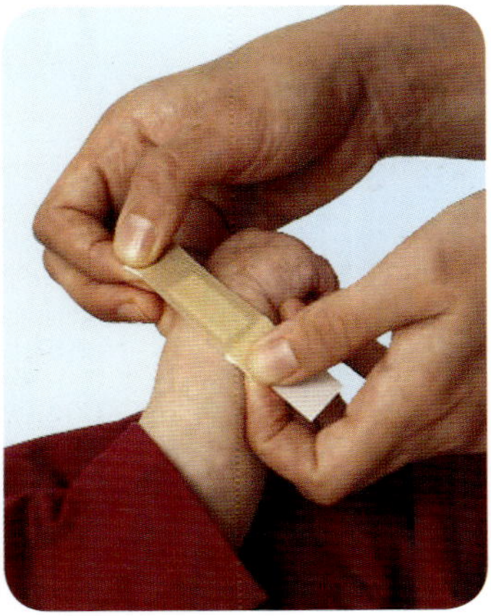

Your nesting instinct

There is nothing like late pregnancy to inspire all sorts of new feelings, including the mysterious "nesting" instinct, which can be alien to women who have previously shown no interest in housework. But go with it! Not only will your home be ship-shape by the time you have your baby in your arms, but you're likely to spur your labor along, too.

- ○ **Get your hospital bag packed** (see pages 68–69)—having this ready will prevent last-minute scrambles or having the task hanging over your head
- ○ **Fill out hospital pre-registration forms**
- ○ **Change the beds** and organize the linen closet—you are bound to have visitors over the first few weeks, and it will help to have everything ready
- ○ **Do one of those once-in-a-lifetime spring cleans**; you may never feel like it again, and the energy you exert will ensure that you fall into a deep, restful slumber
- ○ **Consider inviting a few friends** for a day of spring-cleaning—you'll get it done in a flash, and have some company at the same time; what's more, you can ask someone else to do the heavy lifting and bending
- ○ **Now's the time to invest in natural cleaning products**, not only to ensure that your house is squeaky clean, but also so that there are no chemicals around to endanger your new baby's health
- ○ **Open all the windows and air out the house**; clean the rugs, and let the light in
- ○ **Sort your baby's clothes into sizes**, so you don't find yourself digging through piles to find something that fits once the baby is here
- ○ **Give your cupboards a once-over** and check for anything that might be in low supply; chances are you won't get out much in the early days after the birth, so ensure that all the basics are in stock
- ○ **Do the same in the bathroom**, and treat yourself to a lovely, soothing bubble bath at the same time
- ○ **Prepare a few freezer meals**: there can be nothing better than having a prepared, healthy meal on hand when your arms are full with your new baby and you lack the energy to get dinner on the table

- ○ **Stock your fridge** with good postpartum snacks (see page 88)
- ○ **Make a list of everyone you'd like contacted** after the birth
- ○ **Prepare your birth announcements**—address and stamp envelopes, or design something that can be sent via the internet, slotting in your new baby's photo and details at the last moment
- ○ **Produce something creative**—paint your baby's nursery, cross-stitch a little pillow or picture, start a scrapbook, or simply write a letter to your baby to put in a keepsake box
- ○ **Spend some time finding good online sources** for baby necessities, or create a new "baby" shopping list at your favorite online grocer—when time is tight, all you'll have to do is press a button
- ○ **Consider investing in a diaper service** if you are thinking about using reusable diapers
- ○ **Get your finances in order**—pay outstanding bills, and budget for the coming months (see pages 14–15); you won't want reminders causing you stress when you are busy with your baby
- ○ **And don't forget to make time for yourself**—schedule a manicure, pedicure, or massage; not only will time be tight after your baby arrives, but money may be, too
- ○ ....
- ○ ....
- ○ ....

Preparing for the birth

Labor and delivery options

Giving birth to your baby is a momentous experience. Below are some of the factors you will need to consider when choosing where you want to give birth to your baby, and also when thinking about the type of birth you would prefer to have.

Hospital birth

- **In most cases, you'll deliver your baby at the hospital** where your healthcare provider has admitting privileges; some practitioners have admitting privileges at more than one institution—if this is true for your healthcare provider, ask her how where you'll deliver will be determined
- **Ask questions if you have a choice of hospitals**—for example, investigate the intervention and caesarean rates
- **Find out about hospital policies** on things that matter to you, such as breastfeeding, visitors in the labor ward, your partner being able to stay over with you, and continuity of nurse care

Home birth

- **You can often choose this if your pregnancy is uncomplicated**, and you are in good health
- **In most cases, home births are organized and overseen by a midwife** (see page 73), who must be certified and professional
- **Your caregiver will need to have all of the essential equipment** for your birth, and to begin emergency treatment if there are complications
- **You or your midwife must arrange for emergency back-up** with a doctor or a nearby hospital in the event that things don't go according to plan

Doula

- **A birth doula is a trained labor coach** who will guide you through childbirth and beyond; she will deal with all non-medical aspects of your healthcare, but will not be involved in delivering your baby
- **You also need to arrange for a physician or midwife** to deliver your baby

Birth center

- **If you are keen on a natural childbirth** with plenty of personal attention, this may be the choice for you
- **Birth centers are not widely available at present**, although in rural areas they tend to be more common; some are attached to hospitals, and others are not affiliated with any particular hospital, and run by midwives and/or obstetricians and doulas
- **Some birth centers are covered by your usual health insurance**
- **Some birth centers screen candidates** to ensure that there is a low-risk of complications or problems
- **Birth centers do tend to have at least some modern technology** and are usually equipped to deal with emergencies, but you should be prepared to be transferred to hospital in the event of problems
- **Always check the facilities** to be sure that the midwives and nurses are correctly registered, and that the center is regularly inspected

Types of birth

- **Vaginal birth:** the most common method of childbirth, it's recommended in most cases; women who give birth vaginally can breastfeed more easily, do not need a long stay in hospital and usually heal more quickly
- **Caesarean section:** surgical removal of your baby, during which the abdomen and uterus are cut open to remove the baby; there are a multitude of side-effects, but this may be necessary if you are carrying multiple babies, have a baby in an awkward position, or have some health conditions. Caesareans can also be "elective" in some hospitals
- **Natural birth:** with little or no conventional medical intervention
- **Water birth:** undertaken in your home, some hospitals or birth centers, you will use a birthing pool (tub) during labor and give birth to your baby in the water, or on the surface. Your baby's condition is monitored using a special Doppler device. Check with your hospital, which may have a tub on site, or know where you can hire one
- ....
- ....

What to ask on your hospital visit

As part of the prenatal buildup to the delivery of your baby, you may be offered a tour of the hospital, which is an opportunity well worth taking. Not only will you be able to see firsthand where you are likely to be delivering your baby, but you'll have the opportunity to ask questions about issues such as:

- ○ **Parking, shopping, and cafeteria facilities** (and cost)
- ○ **Admissions procedures**
- ○ **What you'll need to bring**; and what you aren't allowed to bring
- ○ **Visiting hours for friends and family**, the number of visitors allowed, and the policy on young children visiting
- ○ **How to arrange for a private room**, if available
- ○ **The number of mothers per ward**, and whether babies are encouraged to stay with their mothers
- ○ **How the hospital deals with birth plans**
- ○ **The number of babies born, and the intervention and cesarean rates**
- ○ **Who will be delivering your baby**, and continuity of care
- ○ **Whether there are tubs or showers in labor rooms**
- ○ **What types of pain relief are available**; whether you can bring a complementary therapist or use natural remedies during labor; how long you might wait for an epidural (see page 76)
- ○ **What type of fetal monitoring is available**
- ○ **What happens to you and your baby after the birth**
- ○ **What support is available for breastfeeding**
- ○ **Ask to see** the neonatal intensive-care unit
- ○ **Which forms you can fill out ahead of time** to avoid paperwork on the day
- ○ **Ask anything else** at all that springs to mind, no matter how minor
- ○ ....
- ○ ....

Choosing a childbirth class

Childbirth classes are an excellent way to meet other prospective parents and form a support network that can be extended long after the birth. You'll also learn what to expect during labor and the best methods to cope with pain and discomfort before and after the birth.

- ○ **Private classes are usually smaller**, and encourage friencship among the members; you may take them with a variety of different organizations, at birthing centers or with a private instructor in her home or another location
- ○ **You can normally choose from a variety of different courses**, and some are held at different stages of your pregnancy—early pregnancy courses look at nutrition and dealing with symptoms, for example
- ○ **You can often find refresher classes** aimed at women (or parents) who already have children, offering an opportunity to find out the latest theories and research, and get advice on how to do things this time round
- ○ **Consider carefully the organization running the courses**; while you may be dead set on a natural birth, which is supported by the courses you are taking, you should also be aware of the interventions available and when they may need to be used—not everything goes according to plan
- ○ ....
- ○ ....

Class considerations

Try to make sure that the class you choose includes women with roughly the same due dates, since this will help you establish bonds that may last long after the birth. If you don't have time to attend a full course of prenatal classes, which normally run for six to eight weeks, look into one- or two-day "fast-track" courses that might be better suited to your schedule.

Your birth plan

Your birth plan provides you with an opportunity to focus on the different aspects of your care during labor and delivery. You can make this as detailed as you like; but be prepared to be flexible—very few labors go according to plan, and the most important thing is to have a healthy, happy baby at the end of it all.

Consider and make notes about:

- ◯ **Who you would like to have with you during labor**—and whether you'd be willing for student doctors to attend
- ◯ **Your preferred environment**: dim lights, music, what you'd like to wear
- ◯ **How active you'd like to be**—walking, doing yoga, sitting, etc
- ◯ **How you want your baby's heartbeat to be monitored**
- ◯ **Your pain-relief choices**
- ◯ **Whether you want an IV set up**
- ◯ **What intervention is acceptable to you**, and under what conditions
- ◯ **Your views on induction or acceleration of labor**
- ◯ **The position in which you'd like to give birth**
- ◯ **Your views on episiotomies or tearing**
- ◯ **Whether you want to be touching the baby's head as it crowns**
- ◯ **Whether you want your partner to cut the cord**
- ◯ **Your views on taking photographs of the event**
- ◯ **Whether you want to have your baby placed directly on your belly** before he is cleaned and tested
- ◯ **Whether you want to help wash your baby yourself**
- ◯ **What you would like to do with your placenta**
- ◯ **If you know you are having a Caesarean**, you can ask to be awake during the procedure, have your partner there, and have the screen lowered to watch your baby's delivery
- ◯ **How you'd like to feed your baby**

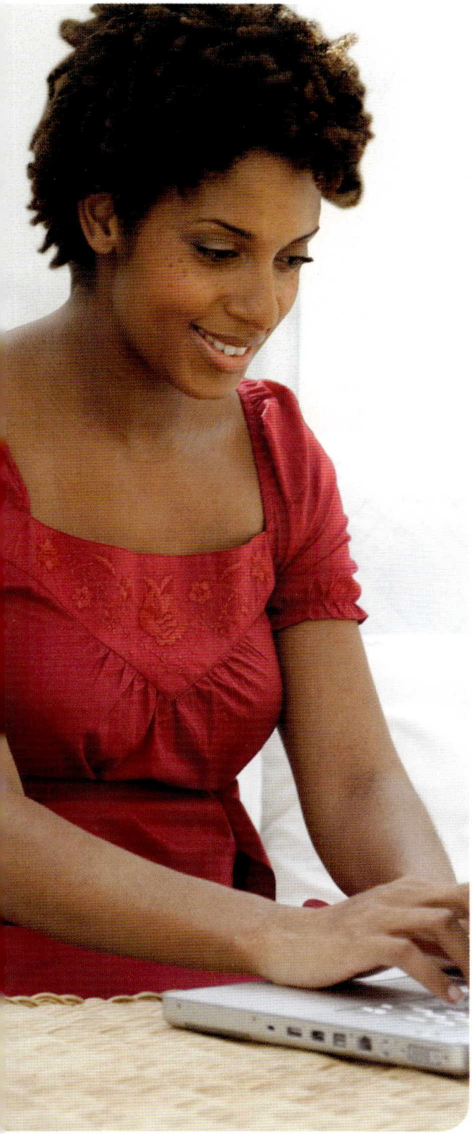

Once your plan is made:

- ◯ **Show it to your doctor and ask her advice**—she'll be able to help you with any information you need, and point you in a new direction if any choices are unrealistic for you
- ◯ **Star or highlight the most important elements**; you may need to change your mind, but if something is important to you, your caregivers should know
- ◯ **It's also helpful to make a list of things** you would consider in every possible circumstance, to give your doctors options
- ◯ **Make copies of the plan** and give them to your birth partner, your doctor, and the delivery nurse attending you at the hospital
- ◯ ....
- ◯ ....
- ◯ ....
- ◯ ....
- ◯ ....

Your hospital bag

It's a good idea to get your hospital bag packed a few weeks before your baby is due, so that you are ready when she is. Always pack a little more than you think you may need in the event that your stay is longer than planned. Remember that your birth partner will look after some of the details (see page 70), so stick to the basics.

- ○ **Your birth plan**
- ○ **Items to help make your environment more personal**, such as photographs or your own pillows
- ○ **A robe**, slippers, and socks
- ○ **An old T-shirt or nightgown for labor**; 1–2 front-opening, clean nightgowns or pajamas for after the birth
- ○ **Lip balm**
- ○ **Snacks and drinks** (if allowed), including bottled water and a drinking straw
- ○ **Toiletries** makeup, hair brush, toothbrush, and toothpaste
- ○ **Any regular medication** (check with your doctor if you plan to breastfeed)
- ○ **Relaxation materials**: a book or magazines
- ○ **Any pain relief**, such as handheld back massagers, TENS machine, a reflexology guide, etc
- ○ **A nursing bra**, breast pads, and nipple cream
- ○ **Old or disposable underwear**
- ○ **Earplugs**, for a noisy ward
- ○ **Your cell phone** (if allowed), or your address book and change for making calls on the pay phone
- ○ **Something to wear home**
- ○ ....
- ○ ....
- ○ ....

Your baby's hospital bag

Although your hospital or birthing center will likely provide you with almost everything you need for your new baby during her stay, you will need to put together a few items to get her home. You may also wish to bring clothing and things that are personal to you.

- ○ **1–2 pacifiers**, if you plan to use them
- ○ **Organic baby bath gel and/or shampoo**—your hospital will undoubtedly provide this, but you may wish to choose your own natural brand
- ○ **1–2 nightgowns** (for boy babies, too) that provide easy access to the nether regions for speedy changes; many hospitals only provide pajamas
- ○ **Scratch mitts**—many babies are born with very long fingernails, and can inadvertently scratch themselves (and you)
- ○ **A comfort item**, such as a soft stuffed animal or a blanket, which you plan to use in the future to soothe your little one
- ○ **2 "going-home" outfits**—choose styles that are easy to get on and off
- ○ **1–2 pairs of socks or booties**, if your going-home outfit is "footless"
- ○ **1 sweater, jacket, or snowsuit**, dependent on the weather
- ○ **1 soft hat or bonnet**, to help conserve your baby's body heat
- ○ **Several diapers**—go for disposables, as you may not have the means to deal with reusables en route
- ○ **1–2 cotton bibs**, for inevitable spills
- ○ **1 pack of disposable, organic wipes**
- ○ **1–2 soft receiving blankets**—large enough to swaddle your baby, or to tuck around her car seat
- ○ **1–2 burp cloths**, for mopping up and protecting your clothes (chances are she'll need to be fed before you get her home)
- ○ ____________________
- ○ ____________________
- ○ ____________________

Your birth partner's checklist

Your birth partner will not only have the honor of being present when your new baby is born, but also some responsibilities as well. Don't feel that you have to organize everything yourself—pass this checklist to your special person, and get him or her involved from the outset. Take a step back and delegate. This list is for your partner's eyes only.

In advance

- ○ **Read up on pregnancy and the stages of labor**, so you are prepared
- ○ **Visit the doctor** with your own list of questions
- ○ **Attend the hospital visit with your partner**
- ○ **Plan and practice a route to the hospital**
- ○ **Review your partner's birth plan**, and find which points she is prepared to compromise on
- ○ **Attend at least one prenatal class with your partner**, to get a handle on the positions and breathing techniques that will help her through labor
- ○ **Make a list of the drugs or other interventions** that your partner is prepared to consider
- ○ **Pack your bags and prepare** as much as you can at least two weeks before the baby is due
- ○ **Make a list of things you need to add to the bag at the last minute**
- ○ **Review the hospital bag checklist** (see page 68) and other Preparing for the birth checklists

Taking charge

Once the contractions have started in earnest, your partner will likely want and need you to take over; so be prepared to call the doctor if her water breaks, or if her contractions are less than 10 minutes apart. Once you arrive at the hospital, brief the delivery nurse on your partner's birth plan, and ask her to show you where to find anything you may need.

Bring along

- ○ **Any natural remedies**, with a note of when they can and should be used
- ○ **Some change for phone calls**; not all hospitals will allow the use of a cell phone; you may also need some change for parking
- ○ **A list of the people you will need to call as soon as baby is born**
- ○ **A camera or video recorder** (if video is allowed), and your battery charger
- ○ **A change of clothes**—labor can be messy
- ○ **Your own toothbrush** and other essential toiletries
- ○ **Games or a deck of cards**, for slower periods
- ○ **Ambient or meaningful music** to play during labor and birth
- ○ **Sandwiches and/or other snacks (if allowed)** and bottles of water to keep you and your partner going
- ○ **A watch or a clock** to time contractions
- ○ **Your partner's hospital bag**
- ○ **The baby's hospital bag**
- ○ **A car seat to take baby home**
- ○ ....
- ○ ....
- ○ ....
- ○ ....

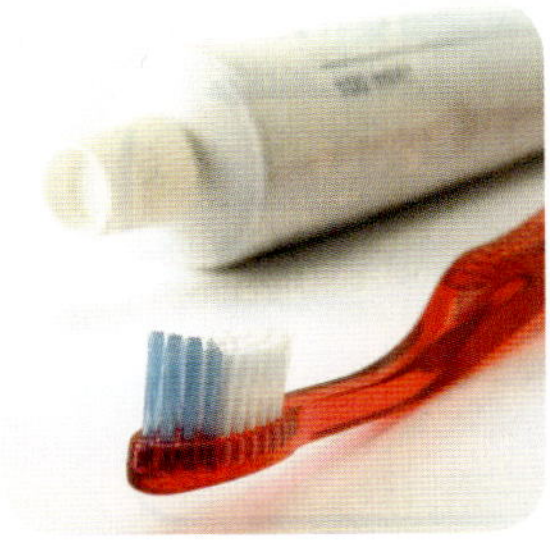

A home birth checklist

Just as you need to prepare your hospital bag well in advance of your due date, it also makes sense to have everything ready for your home birth by at least 36 weeks. Not every baby is tuned into his EDD! A home birth offers you the chance to create the environment you want, so have fun setting it up. You will need the following:

- ○ **Your birth plan**—your healthcare provider may end up being someone new, and it's best to have everything written down
- ○ **One or two plastic sheets** to protect your bed, floor or couch
- ○ **Soft coverings**, such as old towels or sheets
- ○ **Music or candles**—to create the environment that you want
- ○ **Ice cubes**
- ○ **Any pain relief you've organized**, such as a TENS machine, homoeopathic remedies, or a hypnosis tape
- ○ **A hot water bottle or a heated pad**
- ○ **Light, delicious snacks and drinks** to keep you going
- ○ **If you are planning a water birth**, as many old towels as possible
- ○ **Disposable bed mats** (designed for incontinence), which are the perfect size for birthing and for keeping your baby warm
- ○ **Garbage bags for dirty linen**, and the other bits
- ○ **Tin foil**—this is the best way to keep baby warm when he arrives
- ○ **A Tupperware or old ice cream container** for the placenta
- ○ **A bit of ribbon or something special**, if you wish to tie your baby's cord in your own way
- ○ **A warm blanket** to keep you cozy after the birth
- ○ **A clean, front-opening top** for after the birth
- ○ **A "just-in-case" box**, which should include items for you and your baby in the event that a trip to the hospital should be necessary
- ○ ______________________________
- ○ ______________________________

Choosing a midwife

Midwifery care is becoming increasingly common in Canada, and in some provinces and territories it is both regulated and paid for by the heath system. Midwives work closely with the medical profession to be sure that you get the best possible care during pregnancy and beyond.

- ○ **Most midwives have a little more time on their hands**, and you can expect longer and more in-depth antenatal appointments
- ○ **Most women will develop a close relationship with their midwife**, who will often be part of a team that will oversee your birth and care for you and your baby for six weeks after he's born
- ○ **Many midwives are happy to visit you in your home**
- ○ **It's very important that you have a good rapport with your midwife**, and share the same philosophies of childbirth—you will be spending a lot of time together, and sharing one of the most intimate moments imaginable
- ○ **Contact a midwifery practice** as soon as you are pregnant, as they book up quickly; you can, however, opt for midwife care a little later in pregnancy, or choose one to oversee your birth and the postpartum period
- ○ **Check the provision for midwives in your province** or territory—in some areas you will have to pay
- ○ **Make sure you visit the midwifery practice before making a decision**, and ask questions to be sure that it is set up to meet your individual needs
- ○ **Check to find out your birth options**—some midwives have hospital admitting privileges, and are affiliated with one or more particular hospitals, while others may undertake your care in a birth center or at home
- ○ **Most midwives are set up to organize home births** if your labor and birth are likely to be straightforward, and you have not experienced any pregnancy complications
- ○ **Make sure you ask for references**—your family doctor or friends may have a list of recommended midwives, or your local hospital can provide you with details of midwives who have privileges there
- ○ **For more information**, contact the Canadian Association of Midwives
- ○ ....
- ○ ....

Symptoms of labor

Toward the end of pregnancy many women experience Braxton Hicks (or practice) contractions, which can easily be mistaken for the real thing. Before you find yourself rushing to the hospital, check this list to be sure you've passed the real starting line.

Look out for:

- ○ **A profuse emptying of the bowels**, vomiting, or nausea just before your body swings into action
- ○ **Lower back pain**
- ○ **Strong nesting urges** (when you start ironing the tea towels, it's a sign that something's up)
- ○ **Cramping** which feels like your menstrual period
- ○ **Regular contractions** that become increasingly close together and painful (although don't be surprised if they stop—this is normal, too)
- ○ **In early labor you are usually able to converse between contractions**, and behave normally
- ○ **Losing your mucus plug**—the collection of mucus that plugs the cervix; this can be bloodstained, and is called a "show"
- ○ **Your water breaking**, which can be a slow drip-drip, or a rush; don't be alarmed by the quantity of water—there's a lot in there
- ○ ....
- ○ ....
- ○ ....

Quick deliveries

While labor can take at least a few hours (and often much more) in most first-timers, some women do experience faster births. If the contractions are coming thick and fast, or you develop a strong urge to push at any stage, call your doctor immediately.

Questions about procedures

Not surprisingly, many women and their birth partners are daunted by the experience of labor and childbirth, and unsure about when they should speak up, and what they can ask. The most important thing is that you feel confident about your care. If you have concerns, make them known immediately, and ask *any* questions that enter your mind.

- ○ **Ask exactly what any suggested procedure entails** and how it's done
- ○ **Ask about how painful it will be**, if there are any risks to your baby, and any general side effects
- ○ **Ask about the alternatives**
- ○ **Ask why a particular procedure is being suggested**—and whether it is absolutely necessary
- ○ **Ask if a procedure or intervention is established and traditionally used**, or if it is experimental
- ○ **Ask how a drug or intervention will affect** the progress of your labor, your recovery, and the health of your baby
- ○ **Ask what will happen if your labor is slowed**, or if things do not work according to plan
- ○ **Ask about the pros and cons of a treatment**—these should be spelled out
- ○ **Ask for time to discuss the options with your birth partner**, and for the opportunity to ask more questions—or for a second opinion
- ○ **Ask if you can delay intervention**, and if there is any harm in waiting
- ○ **Ask to be notified if there is anything happening that could affect the health of your baby**, as soon as it happens
- ○ **Ask to be told the cut-off periods for interventions**, so that you can consider them; for example, if you are sure you want an epidural, find out how far in advance you need to ask
- ○ ______________________
- ○ ______________________
- ○ ______________________

Pain-relief options

There is a huge range of pain-relief options available from both conventional medicine and natural therapies. Many women choose to combine these two disciplines, others wish to go as natural as possible, and the remainder will entertain anything going! Let's examine what your hospital or birth center should offer.

- ○ **TENS** (transcutaneous electrical nerve stimulation) may be helpful in early labor. It involves attaching pads to your back, through which a low voltage electrical current is passed, stimulating your body to produce its own pain-relieving substances. It takes about 30 minutes to be effective. Some women find it invaluable; others find it ineffective
- ○ **Systemic or injected narcotics and/or tranquilizers** are administered by needle intravenously or into the muscle of your thigh or bottom. Narcotics side-effects include nausea, vomiting, and drowsiness, and they can affect your baby's breathing and make her sleepy. Tranquilizers don't relieve pain, but they will relax you and can make the narcotics more effective. They can make you feel drowsy and out of control, and they may affect your memory of the birth
- ○ **Epidural anesthesia** involves bathing the nerves that run through your lower back between your uterus and birth canal and your brain with a local anesthetic. A fine tube is placed in the region of the nerves, and a painkiller is injected and topped up as required. Once the tube is in position, you will not be aware of it. In a standard epidural your legs will feel quite heavy; a combined spinal epidural (CSE), known as a "walking epidural," allows you to move a little more but isn't available everywhere. You can suffer from headaches or low blood pressure during and after an epidural, but there are very few other symptoms and your baby should not be affected
- ○ **Spinal block** is given as an injection in the lower back, but unlike an epidural, it is injected into the spinal fluid, so the needle is inserted a little deeper (although it does not touch the spinal cord itself). Because the effects of the drug do not last long, and because a spinal block is usually given only once, this form of anesthesia is best suited for pain relief during delivery (not labor), particularly if forceps or vacuum extraction is needed
- ○ ....
- ○ ....

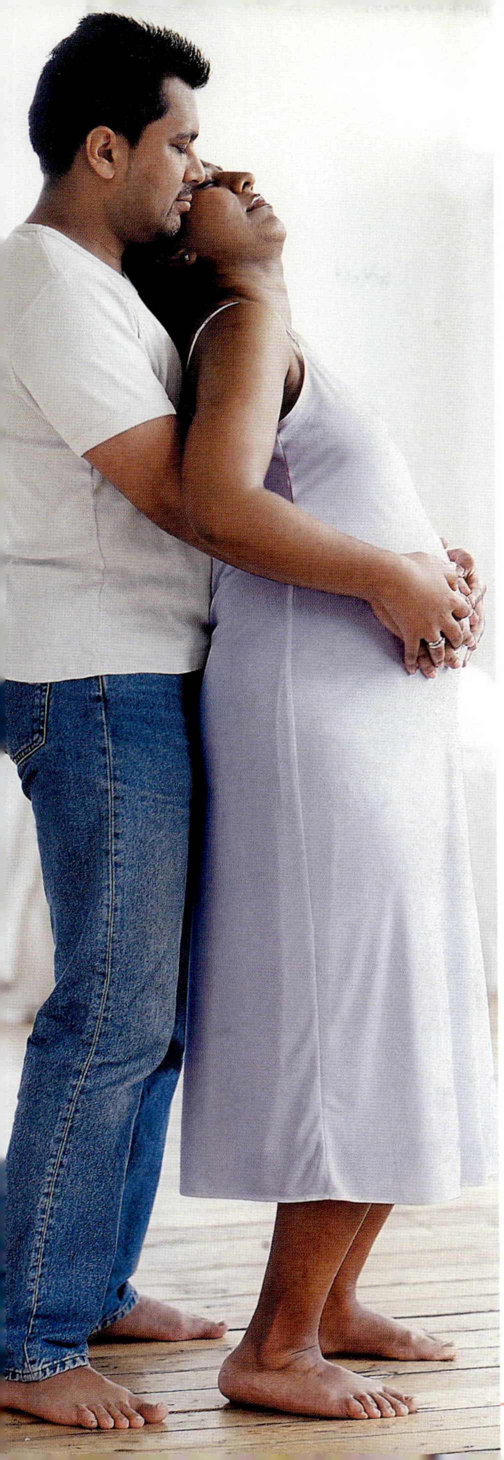

Self-help pain relief

Pain-relief methods that don't involve drugs include: massage (by your partner or a friend), relaxation and breathing exercises (which you should learn at prenatal classes), and water (in a bath, shower, or birthing pool). Gentle exercise, such as walking, bouncing on an exercise ball, or even simple yoga, also helps. In addition, there are a variety of natural therapies that many women find effective, including reflexology, aromatherapy, homeopathy, herbalism, acupuncture, and hypnosis. You can arrange for a therapist to create a remedy kit, to deal with the various stages of labor, to provide you with advice and treatment in advance, or to accompany you during your labor. Always choose a registered, experienced practitioner.

Your gift wish list

More and more parents-to-be are registering for specific gifts in advance of the birth, or putting together a "gift wish list" on one or more websites or at department stores. Not only does this ensure that you get exactly what you need, but it also gives people the option to pool funds for a larger item that they know you want.

Great ideas for your gift wish list can include:

- ◯ **Baby monitor**
- ◯ **Stroller and/or car seat**
- ◯ **Changing table**
- ◯ **Music box or mobile**
- ◯ **Baby sling**
- ◯ **Clothes** (choose various sizes)
- ◯ **Activity center**
- ◯ **Bath towels**
- ◯ **Diaper bag**
- ◯ **An instructional baby massage video**
- ◯ **Baby CD player** and a selection of soothing and stimulating music
- ◯ **Photo session** for the new family

...and not everything has to cost money:

- ◯ **A night's free babysitting**
- ◯ **A meal or two for the freezer**
- ◯ **Housekeeping help** or an ironing session
- ◯ ....
- ◯ ....
- ◯ ....

Visitors and support

To get through the early days of life with your new baby, it can be an enormous help to have a good support network set up in advance. But remember that while helpful friends and another pair of hands can be useful, you'll also need some time alone with your partner and baby.

- ◯ **Set up a visiting schedule**, so you aren't inundated with guests arriving at the same time
- ◯ **Encourage guests to call first** to agree a good time to drop by
- ◯ **Try to limit the number of guests you have in the early days**, and make sure that they are pre-warned that visits will be short
- ◯ **If friends ask to help**, suggest they come for a few hours in the afternoon, perhaps to help get a meal on the table and hold your baby while you get some much-needed rest
- ◯ **Consider putting a list on the fridge**, in bold letters, saying something like: "If you'd like to help…" and listing the things that would be useful
- ◯ **Welcome all offers of meals**
- ◯ **If you have other children, make sure they don't get lost in the excitement**, or that the stream of visitors doesn't disturb their routine
- ◯ **While some thoughtful visitors may remember to bring a small gift for older siblings**, some will forget, so you may want to put some treats by for these occasions to alleviate hurt feelings
- ◯ **Some families find it easier to organize an open-house party** to get the visiting over and done with; make sure it's on a pot-luck basis, and use paper plates for easy cleanup
- ◯ ....
- ◯ ....

Help at hand

Make sure you keep handy the number for your local lactation consultant and pediatrician, so you can ask for advice as you need it.

Your new baby: after the birth

Choosing a pediatrician

If this is your first baby, you will need to find a pediatrician to care for her throughout her childhood. There are many fantastic, experienced doctors around, but you'll need to do some homework to ensure that you find someone who shares your approach to health and well-being.

- ◯ **Ideally, you should begin the search in the final months of pregnancy**; but even at the last minute, your caregivers at the hospital or your own doctor should be able to recommend a pediatric practice
- ◯ **Ask around**—personal references from friends are a great way to start
- ◯ **Before you visit a doctor**, check with the College of Physicians and Surgeons for your province, or the Department of Health and Social Services of your territory, to make sure his or her record is clear of disciplinary actions
- ◯ **He or she should be knowledgeable** about child development and illness prevention, and able to answer your questions fully
- ◯ **Look for an open mind**—you will have your own ideas about how to deal with minor health problems; it's helpful for a pediatrician to share some of your views, and provide different perspectives on other issues
- ◯ **Warmth, compassion, and understanding** are essential
- ◯ **Check that your insurance covers the pediatrician** you want to use
- ◯ **Interview** all the prospective candidates
- ◯ **If there is more than one office** or your pediatrician has partners, will you always have access to him or her?
- ◯ **Check out the office**—is it clean, friendly, and appropriate for babies? Are the staff helpful and friendly? Are there separate areas for well and sick kids?
- ◯ **Check the office hours**—If the office closes early and on the weekends, it might be impossible to schedule appointments that work for you
- ◯ **Ask how middle-of-the-night illnesses and emergencies are handled**
- ◯ **Above all, is this pediatrician someone you can trust** to steer your baby through a healthy childhood, and make the right decisions for him? Go with your instincts on this one...
- ◯ ______
- ◯ ______

Postpartum checks and tests

Your baby will be examined immediately after the birth, and then before you are discharged from the hospital. If you have your baby at home, she'll be checked by her pediatrician or your family doctor, and, also your midwife if you have opted for midwifery care. You can also expect regular examinations (see overleaf) as well as a postpartum check with your doctor.

Your baby

- ○ **The Apgar test** is performed at one and five minutes after the birth, rating your baby's color, breathing, behavior, activity and posture out of 10
- ○ **Your baby will be weighed and measured**, and the circumference of her head will be noted
- ○ **Your baby will be given vitamin K**, either by injection or orally, to help her blood clot
- ○ **A nurse will put antibiotic ointment** or drops in your baby's eyes within an hour of birth to prevent eye infections
- ○ **Your baby will be tested for hypothyroidism** (a disease caused by not producing enough thyroid hormone) and PKU (a disease where the body cannot use a natural amino acid important for baby's growth)—a drop of blood will be taken from your baby's heel for these tests
- ○ **Some experts recommend that you arrange** to have screening tests for the major 30 genetic disorders, which can be done from a single blood sample —talk to your doctor or midwife about this
- ○ **Most babies are also screened for MCADD**, a rare condition which affects the way the body converts fat into energy
- ○ **Within 48 hours your baby will be given a top-to-toe assessment**—this involves examining her head, ears and eyes, mouth, skin, heart, lungs, genitals, hands and feet, spine, hips, and reflexes
- ○ **A nurse or your doctor will regularly check your baby's skin and color** (for signs of jaundice) and ask about her diapers to be sure she is having both wet and dirty diapers regularly
- ○ **Your baby's mouth will be checked** for signs of thrush and her eyes will be checked for any infection

- **Your baby's cord will be checked** regularly to ensure it is drying adequately
- **After a couple of days or even weeks**, your baby will be given a full check-up by her pediatrician, and all of the above will be checked again
- **In some regions**, babies have a hearing test done before being discharged from hospital; if you live in a region where this is not done, ask your doctor about having the test done in you baby's first month

You

- **After the birth**, your doctor or midwife will check your uterus to be sure it's firm, and that there are no retained products of the birth
- **Bleeding and discharge will be assessed**
- **Your blood pressure** will be checked
- **A vaginal examination** may be offered if there is abnormal bleeding, problems with vaginal tears or an episiotomy, or unusual pain
- **Your blood will be checked** if you were previously anemic
- **Your urine may be tested** to be sure your kidneys are working properly
- **Your perineum or Caesarean scar** will be checked to ensure it's healing well
- **You'll need to confirm that your bladder and bowel** are functioning properly
- **Breastfeeding** will be discussed
- **Your emotional health** will be discussed, to ensure that you are not at risk, or suffering from, postpartum depression (see opposite)
- **At six weeks, you'll be given a full checkup**—bleeding should have stopped, and your uterus returned to normal size, by this time
- **If you are not immune to rubella** (German measles) and were not given an immunization before you left hospital, you will be offered one now
- **The postpartum or six-week check** marks your official discharge from the maternity services, unless you have complications, which need further visits
- **You may be offered a Pap smear test** at this checkup, and a chance to discuss contraception; if you choose to use an IUD, it may be inserted now
- ....
- ....

Postpartum depression (PPD)

PPD affects about 10 percent of all new moms. The symptoms differ from woman to woman, and it's normal to experience at least some of these after birth. It's important, however, to look out for the following symptoms—be honest with yourself about how you are feeling, and talk to your doctor if you are concerned.

- ○ Lethargy
- ○ Tearfulness
- ○ Anxiety
- ○ Guilt
- ○ Irritability
- ○ Confusion
- ○ Disturbed sleep and excessive exhaustion
- ○ Difficulty making decisions
- ○ Loss of self-esteem
- ○ Lack of confidence in your ability as a mother
- ○ Loss of libido
- ○ Loss of appetite
- ○ Difficulty concentrating
- ○ Hostility or indifference to people you normally love
- ○ Fear of harming yourself or your baby
- ○ Helplessness
- ○ ....
- ○ ....

Allow others to help

There is no shame in suffering from PPD. Rest, take time for yourself, and accept any help offered. Call your doctor if your symptoms worsen after a week.

Getting enough sleep

Having already experienced difficulty sleeping in the last weeks of pregnancy, and then the physically exhausting experience of labor, it can seem daunting to discover that your new baby will offer you little opportunity to rest. But sleep is essential for new moms (and dads), and there are ways to juggle things so that you get what you need.

- **Sleep when your baby sleeps**—if she's a night owl and keeps you up every night, then go with it until you feel energetic enough to try to adjust her routine
- **Forget about housework and all other chores**—it's more important that you rest when you can
- **Try not to feel guilty about spending time watching TV** with your feet propped up while your baby is at your breast, or catching a nap when she dozes off to sleep
- **Don't panic**—you'll need to make a mind shift and forget about the idea of getting seven or eight hours of uninterrupted sleep in a row; if you accept your sleep is going to be broken, you'll feel calmer and less stressed
- **Even 10-minute naps** will help to relieve the sleep drought, and recharge your batteries
- **You may find it hard if you are normally organized and energetic**, but take up all offers of help so that you can rest and sleep
- **Pay a visit to mom and dad** or a kindly friend, who will welcome the opportunity to pamper you and spend time with your little one while you rest

Surviving sleeplessness

One study found that new moms sleep, on average, only four hours a night—and sometimes less if they are breastfeeding—so it's not surprising you're tired. The most important thing you can do is avoid panicking. Try not to watch the clock, which will only remind you of how little sleep you are getting. Fall into rhythm with your baby, and remember, once she's established a healthy sleep cycle, you'll quickly be able to catch up on yours.

- **Figure out who is the owl and who is the lark**—if your partner loves getting up early, then hand over baby after nursing and go back to sleep; if you don't mind late nights, then take over while your partner goes to bed
- **Get organized**—if you get yourself into some sort of a routine, you'll know when you can sleep and when you'll have some time for yourself
- **Finally, pamper yourself a little**: have a long bath scented with relaxing aromatherapy oils then take a book to bed while someone else watches baby—you may only read a page or two, but this time to yourself will help you unwind, and you'll drift into a restorative sleep
- ....
- ....
- ....

Best snacks for new moms

Breastfeeding and the physical recovery from labor and delivery can leave you tired and hungry, so it's important to top up your energy levels with healthy snacks throughout the day. The ideas below will encourage a speedy recovery and improved mood.

- ○ **All of the snacks suggested for pregnancy** (see page 20) are ideal during the postpartum period, and it's a good idea to stock up your fridge and freezer before your baby is due
- ○ **Try to be sure you are getting some omega 3 oils**, found mainly in fish, nuts, and seeds, in your daily diet; studies have found that these oils are great for enhancing brain function and keeping depression at bay
- ○ **Eat plenty of good-quality protein**—this is necessary for your body to produce the neurotransmitter serotonin, which has a calming effect; slices of lean meat or scrambled eggs make excellent snacks
- ○ **Make sure snacktime includes plenty of fresh, hydrating drinks**—herbal teas can be iced and mixed with honey and lemon to refresh, while fresh water is even better; fatigue and anxiety are symptoms of dehydration
- ○ **A little dark chocolate** will give you an energy boost, as well as some iron, without sending your blood sugar spiraling; chocolate is also associated with increased serotonin levels in the brain
- ○ **When you are preparing meals**, cut up some extra celery, carrots, peppers, and broccoli, and keep them in a little fresh water in the fridge—they're great with hummus or other dips
- ○ **Throw some fruit and yogurt into the blender** to make a smoothie
- ○ **Avoid sugary and refined snacks**, such as chips, cookies, and cakes—they may satisfy you in the short term, but your blood-sugar levels will soon plummet, leaving you feeling tired and irritable
- ○ ....
- ○ ....
- ○ ....

Quick family food

Time is at a premium when you have a new baby, so it makes sense to create easy, quick, and healthy family dishes that will last a couple of days, and can even be frozen for later meals. Try some of these:

- ○ **A hearty vegetable soup**, made with a good chicken or vegetable stock, plenty of root vegetables, a handful of savory herbs, and simmered for a couple of hours, will provide a great meal served with bread and cheese
- ○ **Place sliced ham, cheese, coriander, and spring onions in a tortilla**, fold in half, lightly fry or grill until melted, and serve with a bowl of soup
- ○ **Dig out your slow-cooker**—you can drop in some inexpensive cuts of meat or poultry, lots of root vegetables, some wine and stock, and leave it to simmer all day
- ○ **Brown some ground beef**, which can be adapted to make Bolognese sauce, chilli con carne, moussaka, and lasagne; freeze in portion sizes, and defrost when required to create whichever dish you crave
- ○ **Roast a large chicken** and use for sandwiches, curry, soup, or salad
- ○ **Roasted vegetables** with a scattering of herbs or cheese will provide a nutritious and easy meal
- ○ **Make it easy**: there's no reason why bacon and eggs can't be dinner—or try a delicious cheese-and-veggie omelette for a quick anytime meal
- ○ ....
- ○ ....
- ○ ....

For your records

Developmental checkups

Throughout the early years of his life, your baby will have frequent developmental checkups, or "well-child" visits, with his pediatrician. You can also undertake some checks of your own, to be sure that he is reaching his milestones at roughly the expected time.

By 6–8 weeks your baby:

- ○ **Is smiling and following a moving object with his eyes**
- ○ **Can hear and respond to sounds**
- ○ **Has established some semblance of a sleep routine**
- ○ **Doesn't cry excessively**

By 8–9 months your baby:

- ○ **Can sit without support and has good head control**
- ○ **Is developing hand-eye coordination**—can reach and grasp with each hand
- ○ **Can interact socially**
- ○ **Babbles and responds to speech**

By 18–24 months your baby:

- ○ **Is walking** with a normal symmetrical gait
- ○ **Has normal hand function and coordination**
- ○ **Is beginning to use words with meaning**; may put two words together
- ○ **Can understand a lot of what you are saying**
- ○ **Points to request things** or draw attention to something of interest
- ○ ______________________
- ○ ______________________
- ○ ______________________

Weight and length log

The pediatrician's office should weigh and measure your baby and note the details in your child's record at every visit. However, you may also wish to weigh and measure your baby on your own, and keep a record of the changes. Try to use the same scales each time you do so to ensure accuracy.

Date	Age	Weight	Length

Waking and sleeping log

Use this log on a daily basis to track when your baby sleeps and wakes. Not only will it help you figure out her rhythm and identify problem times, but it will also help you to establish when you can get a regular break. Photocopy the log in advance if you think you may want to continue recording once this one is full.

Day/time	How long awake	Time baby fell asleep	How baby fell asleep

Day/time	How long awake	Time baby fell asleep	How baby fell asleep

Immunization log

Each province and territory in Canada has its own schedule of vaccines. Your family doctor will use the schedule for your jurisdiction. Not all vaccines are covered by each of the province/territory health plans and parents have to decide if they will buy certain vaccines that are now recommended. Generally speaking, you can expect the following:

Age	Date	Vaccine
Birth or in pre-teens		HB (hepatitis B)
2 months		DTaP-IPV (diptheria, tetanus, acellular pertussis [whooping cough] and inactivated polio virus), Hib (Haemophilus influenzae type B), Pneu-C-7 (pneumococcal), Men-C (meningitis C)
4 months		DTaP-IPV, Hib, Pneu-C-7, Men-C (meningitis may not be required)
6 months		DTaP-IPV, Hib, Pneu-C-7, Men-C
6–23 months		Inf (influenza)
12 months		MMR (measles, mumps and rubella), Var (varicella [chickenpox]), Pneu-C-7
18 months		DTaP-IPV, Hib, MMR

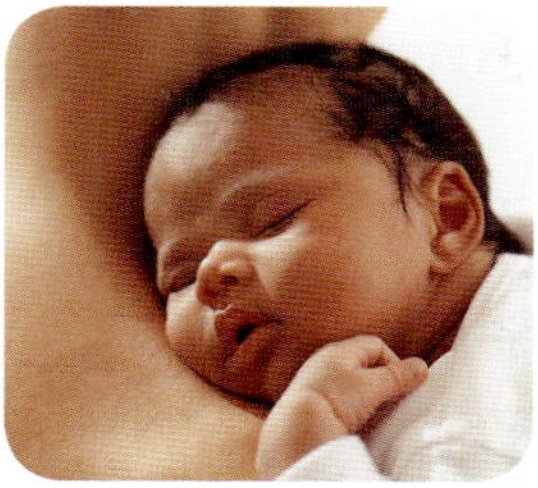

Natural reactions

Many little ones experience reactions to immunizations that can last up to two days. These include a low-grade fever, irritability, drowsiness, and soreness and swelling at the site of the injection. If symptoms persist, see your doctor.

	Where baby was vaccinated (i.e., right thigh)	Vaccination serial number (get this from your doctor)	Side-effects

Visitors, gifts, and thank yous

It's amazing how quickly the first few months of your baby's life will pass, and the details tend to slide into a blur. Use this space to keep a record of visitors and gifts you've received, and check the box when you've written a thank-you note. It will not only help keep you organized, but can also provide a valuable record of those early days.

Date	Visitors	Gift	Thank you sent

Date	Visitors	Gifts	Thank you sent

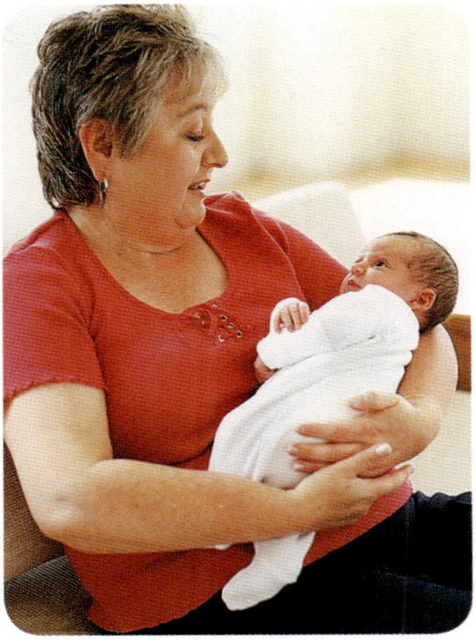

Don't forget...

Make sure you record any gifts you receive while you are out and about, and those that arrive by mail. It's easy to forget things in the early days when you are tired, rushed, and a little hormonal. You'll also find it's nice to have a record of your friends' generosity to look back on once everything settles down again.

Vital records

There are some administrative tasks that need to be taken care of in the first weeks of your baby's life—the sooner the better. You'll need these documents to open savings accounts for your child, add her to insurance plans, and bring her along on your travels.

- ◯ **After your baby is born**, you will receive a form called a Statement of Live Birth from the hospital or midwife
- ◯ **While you are in hospital** you will complete this form, which is then checked and processed by the hospital's administration department, before being sent off to the department of vital statistics (or the registrar general's office) for your province—once your baby is registered, you can apply for the birth certificate and Social Insurance Number
- ◯ **If you have your baby at home**, you will also receive a statement of live birth, provided you were cared for by a registered midwife or doctor—you can then register her birth through provincial authorities; ask your doctor or midwife for details, or ask your local hospital for help
- ◯ **In most cases, the hospital will issue a "souvenir" birth certificate**, but this is not a legal document, and you will need a certified copy
- ◯ **Parents of newborns in Alberta, British Columbia, and Ontario** can now get convenient bundled services from Service Canada and its partners, Service Alberta, the British Columbia Vital Statistics Agency and Service Ontario. You can use the Newborn Registration Service to complete your child's Birth Registration and apply for your child's Social Insurance Number card. In British Columbia and Ontario, you also have the option to apply for your child's Birth Certificate
- ◯ **Check with your provincial or territorial government** for the procedures specific to your area

Health plan cards

- ◯ **When you receive your child's birth certificate** you will, in most cases, need to register your child for your provincial or territorial health plan
- ◯ **In some provinces or territories**, your midwife or doctor will provide you with a health plan application form, which will give you a copy of the number that will eventually be allocated to your baby

Passports

- ○ **Your baby will need her own passport** if you wish to travel abroad and, in some cases, even travel by air
- ○ **One parent** (who must be named on the birth certificate) must complete the appropriate form for children, but both parents must sign it
- ○ **You will need your baby's full birth certificate** (not a card, or the souvenir version supplied by the hospital)
- ○ **There are very specific requirements** for your baby's passport photo, so make sure you read the application carefully before arranging to have her photo taken

Your baby's doctor

- ○ **When you have made your choice of pediatrician** (or family doctor) for your baby, you will be requested to fill in some forms after the birth, to establish her records
- ○ **You will need a health plan card** for your baby, but you should be issued with a number after her birth so that you can visit the doctor before the card arrives; in some jurisdictions, you can use your health card for your baby's first visit to the doctor
- ○ ....
- ○ ....
- ○ ....

Safe storage

Purchase a box folder or accordion filing system to keep all your baby's important documents in one place. You can also keep small mementos here, according to date. It's a good idea to scan key documents and keep them on your computer, in the event that something important is lost or stolen.

Baby basics

Bathing your baby

Although it may sound straightforward, bathing a reluctant, slippery baby can be a challenging experience. The best advice is to make bathing a part of your baby's regular routine, and she'll soon get used to it, and even come to enjoy it—as will you. Follow these guidelines:

- ○ **When she's small**, use a clean kitchen or bathroom sink, or a plastic baby bath—this will make her feel confident, and also protect your back
- ○ **Newborns don't need a daily bath**—spongebathing, or "topping and tailing," (see page 106) in between full baths is just fine
- ○ **Stay calm and don't panic if your baby wriggles**—bathtime takes practice
- ○ **Don't fully submerge your baby until her umbilical cord stump falls off**
- ○ **Run the water before you put your baby in**, and, if you have a single tap, flush it with cold water so it is not hot to touch, and won't drip hot water
- ○ **The water should be no hotter than 100°F (38°C)**
- ○ **Never, ever leave your baby or small child unattended**, even for a second
- ○ **Make sure you are well prepared**—lay out her towel, washcloth, diaper, clean clothes, and baby lotion in advance (but out of splashing distance)
- ○ **Slip your baby into the bath feet first**, and use one hand to support her neck and head, resting them on the palm of your hand or forearm
- ○ **Gently splash or pour plastic cupfuls of warm water** over your baby throughout her bath, to keep her warm
- ○ **Use a thin washcloth** to clean her face; if there are any sticky or hardened bits, gently dab at them rather than trying to scrape them off; add a drop of baby wash to the cloth to clean her neck, torso, behind her ears, between fingers and toes, and her genitals

Bathing together

There's no reason why you can't take your baby into the bath or shower with you. Most babies love it! Just make sure the water isn't too hot, and you don't use any bath or shower products that may irritate her sensitive skin. Having another pair of hands available to scoop her out of the bath first and to dry and dress her can make the experience even more enjoyable and successful.

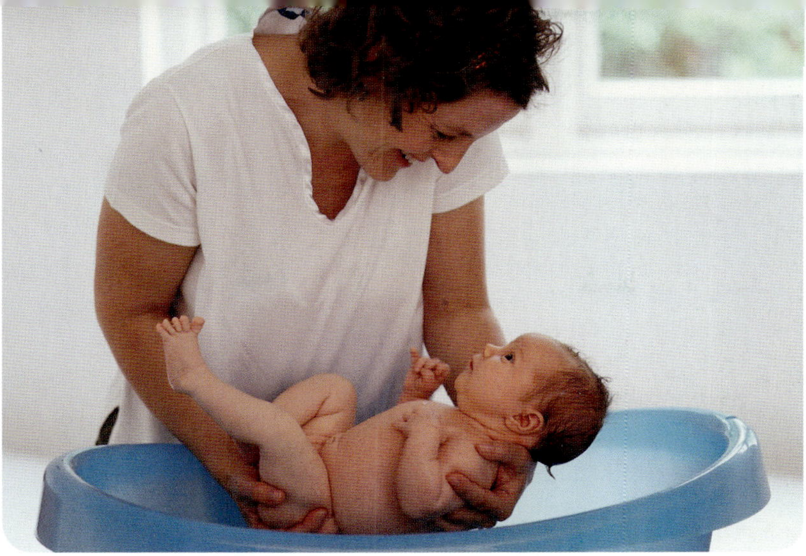

- **Gently turn her toward you** and into the crook of your arm to wash her bottom and back last
- **Wash her scalp or any hair she has** with a drop of baby shampoo, and pour a small cup of clean water to remove the suds
- **Use a cotton ball to clean around her umbilical cord stump**
- **Rinse your baby**, and then lift her out of the bath with one hand supporting her neck and head, and the other under her bottom; hold one thigh firmly with your thumb and forefinger—wet babies are slippery
- **Lift her straight on to a hooded towel**, and pat her dry immediately; if she has dry skin, you may wish to use a very gentle lotion or oil, although most babies won't need anything extra
- **Get her diaper on as quickly as possible**, making sure you have carefully dried the crevices around her genitals and any little rolls on her legs; be aware that babies often urinate just before you get the diaper fastened
- **It's nice to give your baby a cuddle in a dry towel** before you dress her fully—this will help make the bath experience pleasant and memorable
- **Dress her, swaddle her in a warm blanket**, and enjoy her fresh scent
- ......
- ......
- ......

Topping and tailing

Spongebathing, or "topping and tailing," is the ideal way to keep your baby clean before her umbilical cord stump falls off, and can be less traumatizing for bath-shy babies. Small babies don't get dirty on most of their bodies, but they do tend to get messy from feeding and in their diaper areas, so washing those areas is essential.

- ○ **Prepare the essentials**: a washcloth, cotton balls, a bowl of warm water, a clean diaper, and clean clothes
- ○ **Fill a sink or basin with warm water**
- ○ **Remove the baby's clothes** and wrap him tightly in a clean, dry towel so that his arms are firmly by his sides
- ○ **Lay him on a flat surface** near the bowl of water and use the washcloth to wash one body part at a time. First dampen the washcloth and gently clean his face, using a fresh corner for each eye, behind his ears, and in the creases of his neck. Unwrap only one body part from the towel at a time to keep your baby warm. Gently bring the washcloth under his arms, across his tummy, down his legs, and between his toes
- ○ **Gently clean around his umbilical cord stump**
- ○ **Gently sit him up**, supporting his head as you do so, and wash his back and the backs of his legs
- ○ **Clean his genital area** and his bottom last
- ○ **On days when you'll be washing his hair**, save this step for last—wet his hair, lather, and rinse
- ○ **Once again, thoroughly dry his genital area first** and get that diaper on
- ○ **Dress him and wrap him tightly**, ready for a clean-smelling cuddle
- ○ ....
- ○ ....
- ○ ....

Changing your baby

Many parents set up a changing table in the baby's nursery, with diapers, wipes, a bowl for warm water, cotton balls, diaper cream, and a diaper pail. You may also choose to set up a mini-station in another part of the house where you spend time feeding and playing with your baby. Keep a spare set of clothes there, too.

- ◯ **Make sure you always change your baby on a firm surface**, and do not let him go, even for a second
- ◯ **In the early days**, it makes sense to dress your baby in easy-to-open clothing, which can be removed with the minimum of fuss
- ◯ **Remember that many babies dislike having their diaper changed**, so coo, smile, and sing in a reassuring voice throughout to help ease any fears
- ◯ **You may wish to hang a distracting mobile** or toy over the changing area
- ◯ **Many babies prefer being washed with warm water** rather than a cold wipe; make sure you get the water ready before you set him down for changing
- ◯ **Alternatively, keep a sealed packet of wipes on a warm (but not too hot) radiator** so they aren't too cold
- ◯ **Remove your baby's diaper and lay it to one side**
- ◯ **With warm water and a thin washcloth or a cotton ball**, gently clean around the genital area
- ◯ **Apply any diaper or barrier cream**, and fasten the clean diaper in place
- ◯ **Check that his undershirt and clothing are clean and dry** before putting them back on
- ◯ **Place the wet or soiled diaper** in the diaper pail; or, if you are using reusables, remove the liner and place it in some water with a drop of detergent to soak
- ◯ **Pour out the water you've used**, and drop any dirty or wet clothing into your baby's laundry basket
- ◯ ....
- ◯ ....
- ◯ ....

Your diaper bag

It's a sensible idea to keep your diaper bag fully stocked and ready to go. It takes long enough to get a baby ready for an outing, without having to search for diaper bag essentials. Try to make a habit of restocking when you return home. Every diaper bag will be different, but to help you be prepared for any eventuality, include:

- ○ **3–5 clean diapers**—if you are using reusables, make sure you have plastic pants and liners, too
- ○ **2 plastic bags** for wet clothes, and dirty or wet diapers
- ○ **Wipes**
- ○ **A washcloth**, for emergency all-over washes
- ○ **Diaper or barrier cream**
- ○ **1–2 changes of clothes**
- ○ **1–2 small boxes or cans of ready-made formula** (if you use it)
- ○ **1–2 clean bottles with lids** (if you use them)
- ○ **1–2 burp cloths**
- ○ **1–2 bibs**
- ○ **A spare pacifier** or two; keep these in a clean plastic bag
- ○ **A spare sweater or coat and hat for your baby**
- ○ **A small packet of facial tissues**
- ○ **A blanket** for warmth or for when nursing
- ○ **Small toys for distraction**
- ○ **A clean shirt for you**—in the event of a diaper or breast leak
- ○ **Breastpads**
- ○ **A bottle of water and snacks for you**
- ○ ....
- ○ ....
- ○ ....

Creating a routine

Whether to care for a baby on a set schedule or on demand is the subject of considerable debate. The decisions you make should be based on your own lifestyle and views, as well as your individual baby's needs. There is also no reason why you can't combine the two approaches. Here are some points to consider:

- **Forget about routines for the first few weeks**—you need time to bond and get to know each other, and your baby's own routine will slowly assert itself
- **There is no doubt that babies respond well to routines in time**, as they grow to learn exactly what to expect and when
- **Setting up a routine can bring a gentle rhythm** to your baby's days
- **Use a schedule as a guideline**, and don't force it; all babies have fussy days, and there will also be days when you may have appointments or activities that mean you aren't where you should be come nap- or bathtime
- **You can start by taking a walk at roughly the same time each day**—do the same with playtime, reading, singing, and her daily bath
- **Feeding on a schedule** helps you keep track of how much your baby takes in and ensures that she is hungrier at feeds; however, it's crucial to breastfeed on demand to secure a good milk supply, especially in the early days
- **There is no reason why you can't feed on demand** while also figuring out a routine—for example, you can offer your baby a feed when you take a break in the mornings to have a cup of juice or just before she usually has her nap
- **This doesn't mean you can't feed her at other times**; simply offer feeds at the times that work best for you, and she will eventually feed more during these times and fall into a habitual pattern of behavior
- **Scheduling your baby's nap- and bedtimes**, preceded by a bedtime routine that she learns to associate with sleep, can be useful for poor sleepers
- **Try bathing, reading a story, and then feeding before bed**; put her down in her bed when you are finished, say goodnight, and leave her—attempt this routine every night, and she will soon begin to see it as a natural event
- ______________________________
- ______________________________

Vacations and trips

One of the greatest things about new babies is that they are very portable, and many new parents like to take advantage of maternity and paternity leaves to go a little farther afield. Start preparing before you pack by making a list of all the things you need to take, including the items below.

- ○ **Your usual diaper bag**, including a fold-up changing mat and a safe interior pocket for your purse and travel documents, so that you only need to carry one bag
- ○ **A travel crib**, with your baby's usual bedding
- ○ **Your baby's usual blanket for sleep or swaddling**, for comfort and reassurance if in an unfamiliar bed
- ○ **A night light** for nighttime feeding and diaper changes; a converter if the power supply and outlets at your destination are different
- ○ **A baby carrier or sling**, for an easy way to transport your baby when out
- ○ **A light, foldable stroller** that reclines, to ensure that your baby's back is protected, and that he is comfortable; don't forget the rain cover
- ○ **A car seat** for trains, buses, planes, cars, and taxis at your destination
- ○ **Diapers**—allow one for each hour you are in transit, plus a few extra for emergencies and delays; you can usually buy more for the rest of your stay at your destination, but pack enough for two days, to be on the safe side

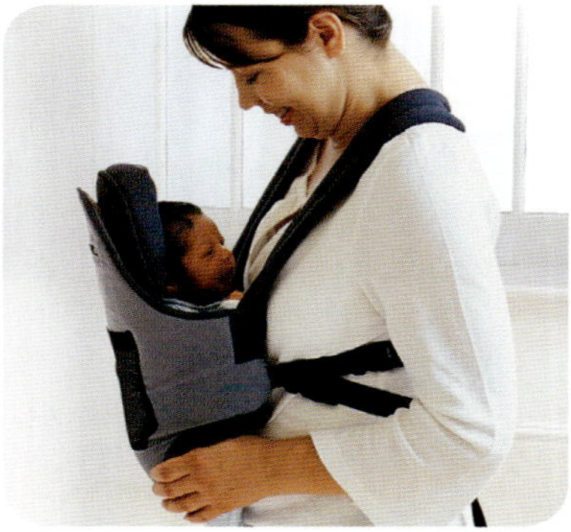

- ○ **Wipes, diaper cream**, and any other baby toiletries you use
- ○ **Tissues**
- ○ **3–4 spare pacifiers**
- ○ **Clothing**: one or two outfits per day; cotton layers are ideal for traveling—socks and sweaters or jackets may be useful, depending on the temperature at your destination
- ○ **Washable or disposable bibs**
- ○ **Plastic bags for dirty diapers, clothes, and bibs**
- ○ **A small bottle of baby's usual laundry detergent**, for emergency washes
- ○ **Sunscreen and a sunhat**
- ○ **2–3 hooded towels**, for bathing and fun in the sun (very young babies should not go into swimming pools or be in strong sun)
- ○ **If you are bottle-feeding**, bring along a full supply of your baby's usual formula, since many babies react poorly to changes in their formula; don't forget bottles, a bottle brush, nipples, and cleaning supplies
- ○ **If you are breastfeeding** you may wish to take your breast pump and some spare bottles
- ○ **Pack an extra shirt** for yourself in your hand luggage, in the event of breast or diaper leaks
- ○ **Baby painkillers or remedies**
- ○ **One or two small toys and books** to help you keep your baby entertained
- ○ **A copy of your list** so you can check that everything returns
- ○ ....
- ○ ....

Clip it on

You may find it useful to take along some elasticated clips to attach extra equipment to your bag or the stroller for days out.

When your baby is ill

Even minor illnesses (see pages 116–119) can be alarming for new parents, but knowing what to look out for will make you much more confident and help you to remain calm when symptoms appear.

Symptoms to look out for include:

- **Fever**
- **Unusually long periods of sleep**
- **Weak or excessive crying**
- **Failure to smile when she normally would**
- **Irritability**
- **Lack of interest in usual feeding patterns**

Be prepared

- **Keep your doctor's phone number by the phone**, and in your mobile phone

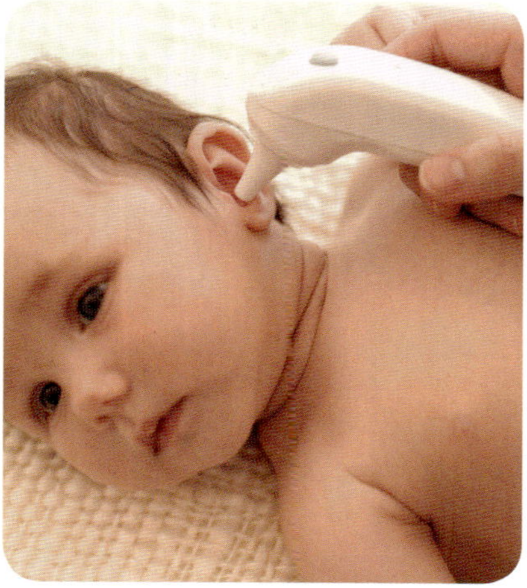

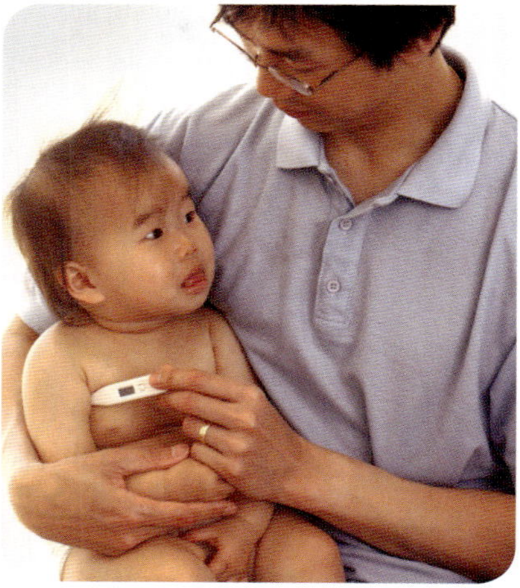

Take your baby's temperature

- ○ **Be aware that body temperatures** vary throughout the day; as a rule of thumb, 100.4°F (38°C) is considered hot for a baby under three months
- ○ **Any baby under the age of three months** with a fever should be seen by a doctor; if your baby is older than this, use your judgment
- ○ **Do not use mercury thermometers**
- ○ **Buy a digital thermometer**: they are fast, accurate, and inexpensive
- ○ **Rectal thermometers** are most accurate for babies and are quick to use
- ○ **Underarm thermometers** are comfortable and accurate, but can take up to 10 minutes to give a reading—use for babies older than three months
- ○ **Oral thermometers** are reliable but, because they take up to two minutes to give a reading, you can end up struggling with a fidgety baby
- ○ **Ear thermometers** are fast, accurate, and easy to use
- ○ **Temporal scanner (strip) thermometers** are placed on your baby's forehead and allow you to take her temperature when she is asleep

Check for signs of dehydration

- ○ **Vomiting and diarrhea are common causes of dehydration**—watch out for these symptoms: listlessness; sunken eyes; dry eyes, mouth, and lips; pallor; fewer wet diapers; darker urine; and a depressed fontanelle
- ○ **Breastfed babies** will need increased feeds, and possibly some additional oral rehydration solution (ORS)
- ○ **Bottle-fed babies** will need ORS with a little formula in between; you may need to continue to offer water and ORS for a few days

And don't forget...

- ○ **To keep your baby warm, but not overheated**—layers are a good idea
- ○ **Keep a close eye on her**—a baby's condition can deteriorate quickly
- ○ **When in doubt, call your doctor** (see page 114)
- ○ ....
- ○ ....

When to see your doctor

No matter what your baby's age or your level of experience, you should learn which symptoms demand a call to your baby's doctor—or, in some cases, emergency services.

Always call your doctor if your baby:

- **Has a stiff neck**
- **Persistently vomits**
- **Is vomiting or has diarrhea** longer than six hours in a small baby, or 24 hours in a baby over three months of age
- **Has a rash on his skin**, particularly if it appears suddenly
- **Is under three months old and has a fever over 100.4°F** (38°C); in babies three months or older use your judgment
- **Has a temperature that is higher than 102°F** (39°C) at any age
- **Has a tender or unusually sensitive or sore-looking belly button or penis**
- **Is suffering from dehydration** (see page 113)
- **Fails to have bowel movements**
- **Has a cold that interferes with feeding**, or with yellow or green discharge
- **Has a persistent or painful cough**, and always if there is mucus coughed up
- **Pulls or tugs on his ears**, and cries when feeding
- **Has discharge from his eyes**

Call an ambulance if your baby:

- **Is floppy, lethargic, and unresponsive**
- **Will not wake up**
- **Has trouble breathing**
- **Has seizures**
- ....
- ....

Baby-proofing your home

Before you know it, your baby will be rolling over and crawling, and even young babies can be hurt if there are hazards in your home. Prevent accidents from happening by making your home as safe as possible as soon as possible—even before he is born, if you can.

- ○ **Make sure your baby's crib has a new mattress that fits snugly**
- ○ **Make sure all screws and bolts are secure**, so there is no danger of the crib collapsing, and your baby won't be scratched if he rolls near them
- ○ **Ensure that there are no strings or electrical cords** hanging anywhere near your baby's bed, changing table, play area, or chair
- ○ **Avoid using pillows, thick bedding, or electrical items** in your baby's crib
- ○ **Keep all lamps and everything else electrical** at least 3 feet (1 meter) from your baby's bed
- ○ **Remove a mobile** from the crib once he can reach up and touch it
- ○ **Consider using a safety belt on your baby's changing table**
- ○ **Put a carpet or rug** at the base of the changing table to cushion any falls
- ○ **Keep small coins, anything sharp, and anything that poses a risk** to your baby (such as choking, strangulation, or injury) out of reach
- ○ **Place all medication, cleaning supplies, alcohol, laundry supplies, and toiletries** in a child-locked cupboard that is out of his reach
- ○ **Place houseplants out of reach**
- ○ **Cover electrical outlets** with plastic covers
- ○ **Install safety gates** securely at the top and bottom of stairways
- ○ **Consider getting a fire guard** if your fireplace is regularly in use
- ○ **Place plastic guards** on the corners of coffee tables and other furniture of baby height
- ○ **Secure bookshelves and chests of drawers to the wall**—many babies become avid climbers very early on
- ○ ....
- ○ ....

Coping with common ailments

Almost every baby suffers from one or more common ailment when young, and it's all part of the process of making the immune system stronger and more efficient. Nonetheless, it can be alarming to see your baby ill, and having the tools to ease her discomfort and put her on the road to recovery can make things much easier.

Reducing a fever

Remember that a fever is a positive sign that your baby's immune system is working effectively, raising the body temperature to make it inhospitable to germs and viruses.

- **Offer plenty of fluids** (see page 113): babies can quickly become dehydrated by intense fevers
- **Offer acetaminophen if your baby is over two months old** or, if she's younger, ask the doctor if it is appropriate—a medicine syringe makes it easier to measure and administer
- **Keep her warm, but make sure she doesn't overheat**—layers of cotton clothing and blankets are best
- **Check your baby's temperature regularly with a thermometer** (see page 113); seasoned parents may be able to detect a fever by feeling their baby's skin, but this is not always accurate enough
- **It can take a few days** for your baby to fight off the infection causing her fever, so keep her comfortable and well hydrated as you both sit it out

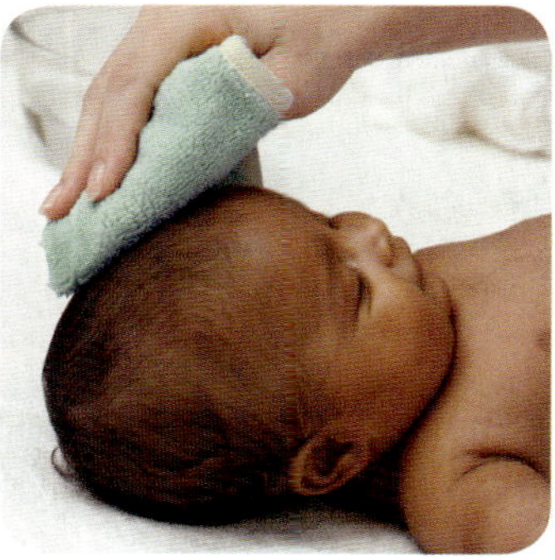

Cooling measures

Sponging your baby with tepid water will help to bring down her fever. Allow the water to evaporate from her skin, rather than drying her, and then dress her in light clothing. If she still feels hot, apply tepid compresses to her forehead, removing them when they absorb some of her body heat.

Croup

The characteristic cough of croup is a definite loud bark or whistle, caused by inflammation of the vocal cords—because the larynx swells and blocks the passage of air, breathing can be difficult, which can panic your baby and you. Croup can be the result of a bacterial or viral infection, or even just a cold.

- ◯ **Raise the head end of your baby's crib** by placing a towel or pillow under the mattress; this should ensure easier breathing
- ◯ **Try steam inhalations** (filling the bathroom with steam is useful) as these will help to open the airways and encourage breathing
- ◯ **Use a cool-mist humidifier** in the baby's room to help keep the nasal mucus more liquid—place it near her so she can take advantage of the additional moisture; clean daily to prevent mold buildup in the vaporizer
- ◯ **Use saline nose drops** (non-medicated) to help loosen the thick mucus in your baby's nose
- ◯ **Your doctor may prescribe** a course of steroids for your baby, which can reduce swelling

Vomiting and diarrhea

These can occur in tandem or on their own. There are a multitude of causes, including gastric reflux, ear infections, coughs and colds (which produce excess mucus), fever, gastroenteritis, and even overfeeding.

- ◯ **Continue offering regular feeds**: bottle-fed babies should be offered plenty of fresh, cool, previously boiled water in a sterilized bottle; you may also want to try a lactose-free formula, which can be more easily digested
- ◯ **Massage your baby with a little warm olive or grapeseed oil**—this will help to soothe her and reduce any cramping or discomfort
- ◯ **Scrupulously clean** everything with which your baby comes into contact
- ◯ **Your doctor may recommend a fluid replacement** (oral rehydration solution) if your baby is suffering from dehydration (see page 113)
- ◯ ....
- ◯ ....

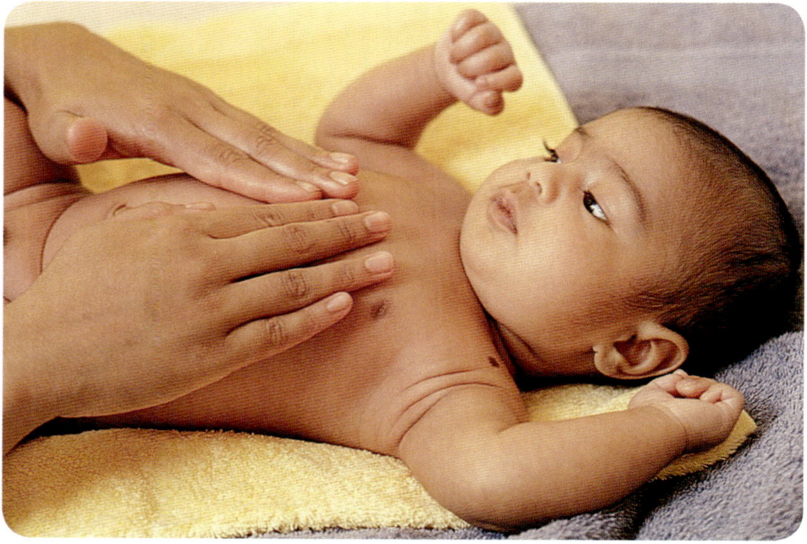

Colic

Colic is characterized by apparently unending frantic crying, usually at around the same time of day or night—your baby will draw his legs up to his abdomen and he will appear to be in severe pain.

- **Remember, if you are breastfeeding**, your baby may be irritated by something you ate and become temporarily fussy; for example, onions, cauliflower, and broccoli can cause your baby to experience gas
- **Note symptoms that appear after feeding** and discuss them with your doctor —babies can occasionally be allergic to foods passing through their mother's breast milk, such as cow's milk or eggs, resulting in an upset tummy
- **Your doctor or pharmacist may suggest anti-spasmodic solutions**, which will reduce discomfort
- **A warm bath** can help to ease symptoms and calm a distressed baby
- **Try a gentle massage of the abdominal area**—do this before the evening feed so that your baby is relaxed and calm
- **Some parents suggest avoiding particular foods**, including very spicy foods, citrus foods, gassy foods (beans, cabbage, onions, etc), and sugar

Colds and coughs

- **A streaming or congested nose and a cough** can make feeding difficult, so keep your baby slightly upright when offering a bottle or nursing
- **Use a vaporizer in your baby's room**, with a few drops of eucalyptus essential oil to help ease the congestion; alternatively, a few drops in a bowl of water on a radiator will help
- **Feed little and often**, ensuring he gets enough without becoming distressed
- **Offer acetaminophen** to help ease discomfort and bring down a temperature

Cradle cap

Cradle cap is characterized by a thick, encrusted layer of skin on your baby's scalp; there will be yellow scales, which form in patches—in severe cases cradle cap can last for up to three years.

- **Massage the scalp with your fingers** to improve scalp circulation and loosen scales
- **Mineral oil** can be massaged into the scalp each evening, and then gently shampooed away after a few minutes to nourish and soothe
- **Alternatively, massage olive oil into the scalp each evening**, and then gently shampoo away in the morning to nourish and soothe; over-washing will make the condition much worse
- **Try not to loosen crusts** that have not pulled away on their own as bleeding and infection may result; gently brush away loosened crusts
- **Your doctor will prescribe** a mild ointment containing an antibiotic and corticosteroid if the skin becomes inflamed or seems infected
- ....
- ....
- ....

Calming diaper rash

Diaper rash results from contact with urine or feces, which cause the skin to produce less protective oil and therefore provide a less effective barrier to further irritation. Almost all babies suffer from diaper rash at some point, and it can be very uncomfortable. Here are some of the best ways to deal with it.

- ○ **Change your baby's diapers more frequently**, and allow her to spend time without a diaper on
- ○ **If you are using cloth diapers**, consider changing to disposables for a while; they tend to be better at keeping urine away from your baby's skin
- ○ **If she continues to wear cloth diapers**, put them through an extra rinse cycle to be sure there are no traces of detergent
- ○ **Don't use baby wipes with alcohol**, which can dry the skin on your baby's bottom—use water and cotton balls instead
- ○ **Avoid using soap or any other detergents** on the diaper area—rinse carefully with clean water at each diaper change
- ○ **Zinc oxide** is an excellent barrier cream for the diaper area, and can also encourage healing
- ○ **After baths, pat the diaper area dry** instead of rubbing, which can further irritate the skin
- ○ **Make sure her bottom dries fully after each cleaning** before you put a new diaper on
- ○ **Try different brands** of wipes, diapers, or baby wash if the rash persists
- ○ **Make sure your baby is drinking enough**, to reduce the acidity of her urine
- ○ **If your baby's rash has white patches**, she may have a yeast infection; antifungal ointments may be prescribed
- ○ **Diaper rash that does not heal** within a week should be seen by a doctor; in very severe cases, your doctor may recommend a mild corticosteroid ointment or cream
- ○ ______________________
- ○ ______________________

Ease the crying

As your baby becomes more settled—usually between six weeks and three months—her crying will change and you will be able to distinguish different cries indicating different needs. Sometimes she may be hungry, or suffering from colic; she may have a diaper rash, or she may be lonely and just want to be held. Here are some tips:

- **Many babies respond to being held and rocked**, although you may find, frustratingly, that something that worked one day may not work the next
- **Babies often like to have their heads near your chest**, in order to hear your heartbeat
- **Rhythmical sounds**, such as low music or even the sound of the vacuum cleaner, soothe babies
- **If your baby is eased off to sleep by rocking,** settle yourself in a position where you can comfortably rock her cradle or swing with a free hand or foot
- **Many babies like to feel securely wrapped**, so you can make her feel more comfortable by swaddling her before settling her down; other babies may feel constrained by swaddles, so a sleep sack will keep her warm
- **Some babies need to suck to get to sleep or to settle**, which is why they feed almost constantly when they are upset—if your baby is not hungry, she may find comfort from a pacifier
- **You can calm her down by giving her a light massage** with a soothing oil
- **Try not to be anxious**—babies have amazing antennae and will respond to your distress in kind
- **You may find that, if you set up a routine that makes her feel secure** (see page 109), she will calm down and feel more comfortable during the day
- **If crying begins after feeding**, after switching from breastmilk to formula, or after a change in formula, talk to your baby's pediatrician—there may be problems with the formula your baby is taking

Stimulating your baby

Almost as soon as your baby is born he will respond to stimulation and enjoy interacting with you. There is plenty of research to suggest that playing with your baby, singing to him, and talking to him can encourage healthy cognitive development and provide the foundation for his budding social skills.

- ○ **Allow your baby to come into contact with** lots of different people, sounds, sights, and other stimuli—what babies see, touch, hear, and smell causes brain connections to be made, especially if the experiences happen in a loving, consistent, predictable manner
- ○ **Talk to your baby constantly**, and give him an early introduction to language; he will be reassured and stimulated by the sound of your voice
- ○ **Take him on "visits"** to different rooms in the house, and outside; show him a bird or a butterfly, or a fast-moving car—everything will be new, and he will be fascinated by the wealth of light, color, movement, and sound
- ○ **Play music** that your baby seems to enjoy, and use his reactions as a guide to what he likes and what he doesn't
- ○ **Give your baby a massage**; the power of touch is well documented, and it will also stimulate him both emotionally and physically
- ○ **Hold his hand under a running tap** and let him run his fingers through the water
- ○ **Sing or read silly rhymes and songs**—this encourages an early appreciation and understanding of language
- ○ **When he's able to hold up his head**, help him to stand up in your lap and bounce a little, which encourages gross motor skills

Meeting milestones

Familiarize yourself with the milestones that your baby should reach in his first year, and plan your games and activities to help him meet them at the appropriate age. This will also help you to make sure that he regularly faces the exciting challenge of doing new things—successfully!

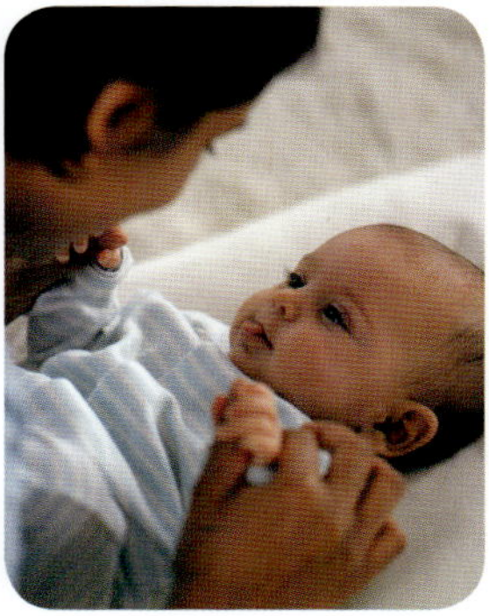  

- ○ **Play peekaboo** with your hands, or hide your face briefly behind a towel or burp cloth
- ○ **Cuddle and hold your baby**—studies show that the more you do this, the more secure and independent he will be when he is older
- ○ **Choose toys that are tactile**, to encourage your baby to become familiar with lots of different physical experiences
- ○ **Jingle keys, shake a box of rice, knock on the table**, and teach your baby a variety of different sounds; he'll soon turn his head to see what's going on
- ○ **Remember that play is crucial** for your baby's social, emotional, physical, and cognitive development
- ○ **If your baby starts to cry during playtime**, switch to calmer activities such as reading from a picture book, quietly singing, or simply feeding—some babies are easily overstimulated
- ○ **Swing a soft toy or ball from the end of a piece of string**, and encourage him to bat or kick at it
- ○ ....
- ○ ....
- ○ ....

Encouraging bonding

Bonding is the intense attachment that develops between parents and their baby. A baby who experiences this attachment fosters a sense of security and positive self-esteem. Here's how it's done.

Bonding with mom

- **Touch is effectively your baby's first language**, so give her plenty of it; babies respond to the smell and touch of their mothers in particular
- **If you are breastfeeding**, you are creating the ideal conditions for mother-baby bonding, with your skin against her cheek
- **If you are bottle-feeding**, hold your baby close to you and let her know that she's safe in your arms; skin-to-skin contact is recommended
- **Eye-to-eye contact** provides meaningful communication
- **Smile at your baby** and exaggerate your facial expressions; even early on she will try to imitate them
- **Your baby will be familiar with your voice** from her time spent in the womb, and she will feel comforted and close to you when she hears you

Bonding with siblings

- **Don't worry if this gets off to a faltering start**—the sibling bond is an intense one, and your new baby will be willing to bond with anyone who loves her and meets her needs, even if your other children are less willing
- **Prepare young children in advance**, explaining that the new baby will need a lot of attention, and probably won't be much fun for a few months
- **Ask your little one to choose a gift** to give to the new baby, and find something your child really wants as a gift from her new sibling
- **Ensure that your children feel loved**, and part of the new-baby experience
- **Involve your children in the care of your new baby**
- **Allow little ones to bathe together**, and spend time naked—they will enjoy this intimate experience
- **Cuddle the new baby and older children together**, so that they feel they are part of the same unit

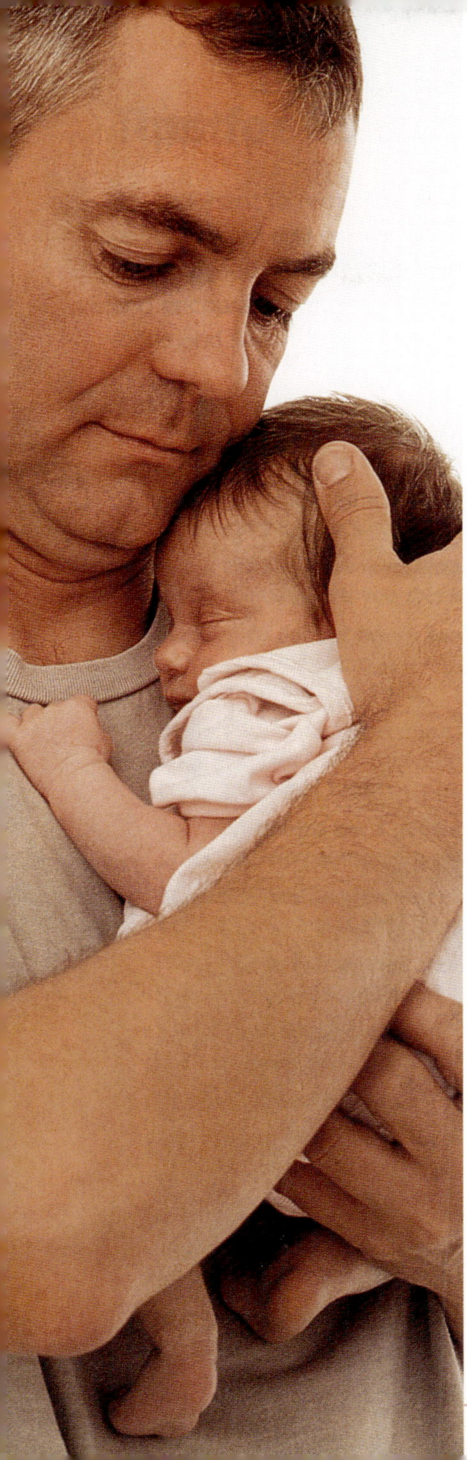

Bonding with dad

- ○ **Be patient. This normally occurs on a different timetable**, mainly because dads don't have the same early contact with their new baby, and also because baby hasn't spent the last nine months sharing the same space with dad
- ○ **It's helpful for dads to set up their own regular routines** with their babies, which establish them as "different" from mom, but equally loving and caring
- ○ **Skin-to-skin contact** can be enormously effective
- ○ **Dads can read or sing to baby**, and share a bath; mimicking baby's cooing or other vocalizations can establish a rapport
- ○ **Carrying baby in a front-loading sling** is a good way for baby and dad to bond, as it lets baby feel the different textures of dad's face
- ○ **If you are bottle-feeding, dad can offer a regular feed each day**; if you are breastfeeding, consider expressing so that he can do an evening feed
- ○ ....
- ○ ....
- ○ ....
- ○ ....

Your baby: 0–3 months

Developmental milestones

All babies develop at different rates, but as long as your little one is reaching her developmental milestones at roughly the appropriate time, you'll have nothing to worry about. Keeping track of her development is not only a source of great pleasure, but also alerts you to any potential problems in plenty of time to set things right.

By three months, your baby will likely be able to:

- ○ **Grasp items reflexively**
- ○ **Lift her head**
- ○ **Suck well** from your breast or bottle
- ○ **Coordinate her sucking, swallowing, and breathing**
- ○ **Smile socially**
- ○ **Stop crying** when she is picked up and held
- ○ **Use a different cry** when she is tired, hungry, or in pain
- ○ **Coo when she is spoken to**
- ○ **Recognize her parents by sight**
- ○ **Visually track moving objects** or faces from 8–10 in (20–25 cm) away
- ○ **Look in the direction of sounds**
- ○ **Move her arms and legs** to show interest in the action around her
- ○ **Bring her hands and fingers to her mouth**
- ○ **Take some of her body weight on her legs** when standing supported
- ○ **Have some semblance of a routine**, sleeping less in the daytime and more at night
- ○ **Control the muscles in her arms and legs** as she starts to grab or kick at toys or people
- ○ ....
- ○ ....
- ○ ....

Best first toys

Your new baby can see only a short distance in front of her face, and she won't see everything in full color for another few weeks; however, her sense of touch and hearing are very well developed, and she will enjoy experimenting with different sounds and textures. Offer her the following toys in her first few weeks:

- ○ **A high-contrast mobile** for her crib or bassinet
- ○ **A light rattle**—wrist or sock rattles are ideal
- ○ **Soft toys that crinkle, ring, or rattle when touched**, with a variety of different textures and surfaces to investigate
- ○ **A washable soft toy**—babies often form attachments in the early weeks that last well into childhood
- ○ **Musical toys**, particularly those that respond to her gentle kicks or touch
- ○ **A baby mirror** placed by the crib
- ○ **Books with pictures or photos** of brightly colored animals, or of faces
- ○ **Books of nursery rhymes**—your baby will love familiar, repetitive songs and stories...and the sound of your voice reading and singing them
- ○ **An automated swing**—your baby may enjoy this for her first six months, not only because she'll feel soothed by the feeling of being rocked, but also because it will entertain her as the world goes flashing by
- ○ ______________________
- ○ ______________________

Breastfeeding basics

Although breastfeeding is one of the most natural acts in the world, it can take a lot of practice before you get the hang of it. Both you and your baby may be amateurs, so take your time to become accustomed to different positions, and enjoy the experience.

- ○ **Experiment with different positions**—some moms like the "cradle hold," while others prefer the "crossover hold" where they use the opposite arm and hand to hold the baby to the breast they are feeding from
- ○ **Ask your pediatrician, OB, or a lactation consultant** for advice about the many different breastfeeding positions, and experiment until both you and your baby are comfortable
- ○ **Regularly alternate breastfeeding holds**—each hold puts pressure on a different part of your nipple and you may find that using different holds is the best way to avoid getting clogged milk ducts
- ○ **Make sure your baby is facing you**, usually lying on his side, rather than on his back
- ○ **You might find it easier if you put a footrest or low table under your feet**, to offer more support and prevent having to bend over your baby
- ○ **Choose a comfortable chair with armrests**, and use a pillow to support your back and arms
- ○ **Always bring your baby to your breast**, rather than the other way around
- ○ **Use one hand to support your breast** as you nurse
- ○ **Try swaddling your baby** or gently holding his arms by his side to make nursing easier
- ○ **Alternate the breast you first feed from**—not only will your baby get the hydrating foremilk before moving on to the rich, more nutritious hind milk, but you'll ensure that both breasts keep producing plenty of milk
- ○ **Try to relax before feeding**
- ○ **Keep a tall glass of water or juice** by your side to keep you hydrated, which helps you to produce milk
- ○ **Ensure that your baby latches on correctly**—this is undoubtedly the secret of successful breastfeeding (see opposite)

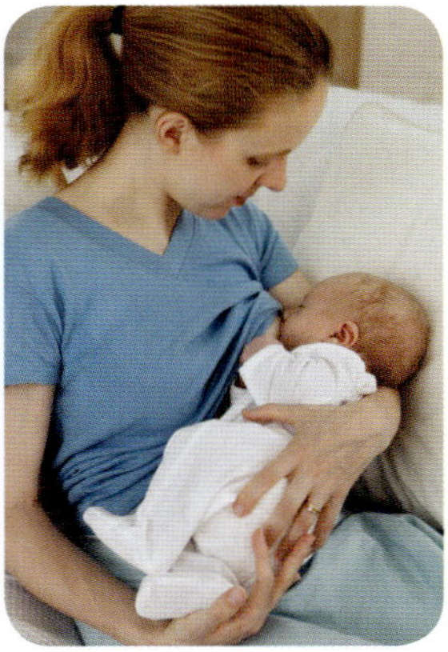

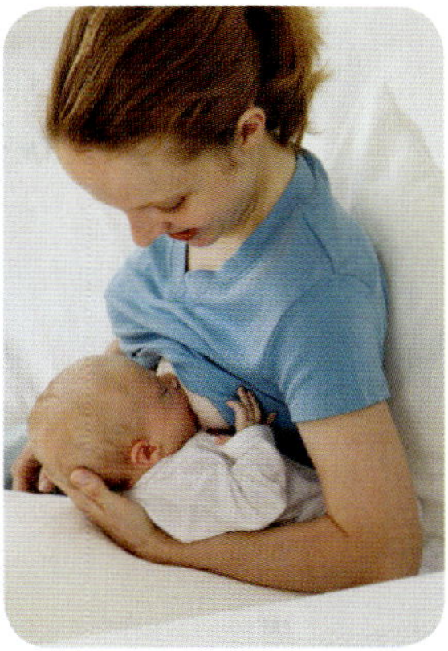

Latching on

- **To help ensure a good latch**, hold your breast and touch your nipple to your baby's nose; tickling his cheek and lips with the nipple will encourage the "rooting reflex," sending a signal to your baby to open his mouth
- **Your baby's mouth needs to be open wide**, with his tongue down and forward, and your nipple should be aimed at the roof of his mouth
- **He should be drawing all of the nipple** and some breast tissue into his mouth, his lower lip will be rolled out, and his chin will be against your breast
- **When your baby is correctly latched on**, you should hear only a low-pitched swallowing noise—not a sucking or smacking noise—and you should see his jaw moving, a sign that successful feeding is taking place
- **To remove your child from the breast**, carefully insert your clean little finger into the corner of his mouth—a gentle "pop" means you've broken the suction and you can pull him away
- ....
- ....
- ....

Breastfeeding problems

Even the most seasoned breastfeeder can experience some discomfort and other problems while feeding. Fortunately, there are plenty of tried-and-tested tricks to help ensure breastfeeding is a success.

Engorgement

- **Check your baby is latched on properly** (see page 131) as this will make sure that all of the breast is emptied of milk and help relieve engorgement
- **If she struggles to get a grip on an engorged breast**, express some milk before feeding—this will also relieve the feeling of fullness
- **Continue feeding from the engorged breast**, which will offer some relief
- **For extreme discomfort, try placing cold, bruised cabbage leaves** in your bra—the enzymes appear to reduce swelling and prevent oversupply of milk

Mastitis

- **You may notice hot or red streaks** on your breast, and experience pain and even a high temperature; mastitis can result from severe engorgement, poor latching-on, or blocked milk ducts (see below)
- **Feed frequently from both breasts**, but especially the affected side
- **Some women have success with homeopathic remedies**, but check with your doctor first to see if the treatment is safe for your breastfeeding baby
- **Try to express milk** to empty the breast and move the lumps
- **See your doctor** if your symptoms don't improve in 24 hours; you may need antibiotics

Blocked ducts

- **The best treatment** for this is regular feeding to get the milk flowing
- **Massage the breast and hand-express milk**, moving the milk down the channels toward the blocked ducts
- **Place warm compresses** over the affected areas, and ensure your baby has the whole nipple in her mouth every time she nurses

Sore and chapped nipples

- **Try to relax** when you are nursing, which will help the milk come
- **Seek advice from a lactation consultant**—poor positioning and latch (see pages 130–131) are the main causes of sore nipples
- **Start feeding on the breast that is the least sore**
- **Try to avoid pulling her off**, since the suction created by her mouth on your breast can make it more painful (see page 131)
- **At the end of a feeding**, express a little of the rich, fatty milk and rub it over your nipple to encourage healing
- **Between feedings**, keep your bra and shirt off for short periods to allow the air to get to your nipples
- **Avoid using plastic-backed breast pads**, and change damp pads
- **There are some good emollient creams** available for sore nipples, many of which contain all-natural ingredients, such as lanolin

Shortage of milk

- **Be patient**: it can take some time for your milk supply to become established and for "supply and demand" to kick in
- **Allow your baby to nurse frequently**, since this will stimulate your body to produce more milk; if necessary, wake your baby to nurse, and also express milk between feedings to help stimulate milk supply
- **Make sure that you are relaxed** when you feed her—if you are tired and anxious, it might seem as though there is no milk, or not enough
- **Take some time to rest**, and even retire to bed with your baby for a day or two, to divert your energy toward making milk
- **Make sure you are getting enough to eat**—you need plenty of energy to produce milk, and an inadequate diet can certainly affect your milk supply
- **Offering both breasts at each feeding** and making your baby do all of his sucking at the breast (no bottles or pacifiers) should help
- ....
- ....

Bottle-feeding basics

Many women can't or don't want to breastfeed. The good news is that formula offers your baby all the essential nutrients he needs and is designed to be as close to breastmilk as possible. There are a few things to bear in mind with bottle-feeding:

- ○ **Carefully follow the manufacturer's instructions**—too much formula powder or liquid can cause your baby to become constipated or thirsty; too little may mean he isn't getting what he needs in terms of nutrition
- ○ **Make up bottles with water that has been previously boiled and cooled**—ideally the water temperature should be 158°F (70°C) or hotter, since formula is not sterile—this level of heat will kill any bacteria in the powder
- ○ **Choose a nipple that is the right size** for the age of your baby, and experiment to see if he prefers faster or slow-flow nipples
- ○ **To feed your baby**, cradle him in a semi-upright position and support his head; don't feed him lying down—formula can flow into the sinuses or middle ear, causing an infection
- ○ **To prevent your baby from swallowing air as he sucks**, tilt the bottle so the formula fills the neck of the bottle and covers the nipple
- ○ **Your newborn will probably take 2–4 oz** (60–120 ml) per bottle during his first few weeks, and he will probably be hungry every two to four hours
- ○ **Don't encourage your baby to empty the bottle** if he's not interested; and if he's still sucking when the bottle is empty, offer him more
- ○ **To prevent a tummy full of air**, burp your baby frequently
- ○ **Thoroughly clean and sterilize bottles, nipples, rings**, and the equipment you use for preparing and cleaning your baby's bottles
- ○ **Do not use mineral water to make up bottles**—it will upset the balance of nutrients in the formula
- ○ ....
- ○ ....
- ○ ....

Soothing your baby to sleep

If there's one source of despair for new parents, it's trying to get their babies to sleep. New babies can be erratic sleepers, and wakeful just when you need sleep the most. Here's some help for harried parents:

- ○ **Babies often jerk themselves awake** (a natural reflex)—you can avoid this by swaddling your baby tightly in a blanket at bedtime
- ○ **The bedtime routine** is one of the most important routines you can establish—when your baby begins to recognize his own routine, he will relax and feel secure, and he will know what to expect
- ○ **Some babies appear to be born with their own body clocks**, and you may notice before he is even born that your baby has periods of activity in the nights, which is a sure sign that you have a night owl on your hands
- ○ **Keep window shades or curtains open while he sleeps in the day** and settle him down for naps at regular intervals
- ○ **If he falls asleep feeding**, gently wake him and spend some time talking to and playing with him
- ○ **Keep household activities as noisy** as possible during the day, so he becomes used to the idea that it's normal to be awake during these hours
- ○ **Put him to bed at a reasonable time**, even if he's not obviously tired; come back if he calls, but don't be tempted to get him back up again
- ○ **Take turns putting him to bed**—your baby will get used to both mom and dad being involved in the bedtime routine and won't kick up a fuss if one of you is unavailable
- ○ **When he wakes in the night**, feed, change, and comfort him, but keep the lights low and talk to him quietly
- ○ **Wake him in the morning at a reasonable hour** and keep things as routine as possible throughout the day—he'll soon learn that daytime is for fun and nighttime is just plain boring, so he might as well go to sleep
- ○ ....
- ○ ....
- ○ ....

Your baby: 3–6 months

Developmental milestones

You will be astonished by how quickly your helpless new baby becomes a confident, eager explorer, able to master all sorts of new tricks. There is no need to push her toward achieving her milestones—she'll get there all on her own. You can, however, offer her a little help when she feels frustrated by her inability to get things just right.

By six months, your baby will likely be able to:

- ○ **Smile frequently**, and she's now starting to laugh
- ○ **Focus on objects** up to 3 ft (1 m) away
- ○ **Follow with her gaze** objects going across, over, and under her
- ○ **Hold her head up** to look around
- ○ **Enjoy looking at and playing with her hands and feet**
- ○ **Push herself up on her hands** when she's on her tummy
- ○ **Begin to try to roll over**—this often starts when she manages a turn accidentally and then learns that she can reproduce it with a little effort
- ○ **Reach and grab things**
- ○ **Play with both hands together**
- ○ **Imitate more facial expressions**
- ○ **Begin using different vowel sounds**
- ○ **Begin squealing**, as she explores the different pitches of her voice
- ○ **Become more active** in getting your attention
- ○ **Begin to sit with support**
- ○ **Show an interest in food** and feeding herself (although she won't be ready for weaning quite yet—see page 144)
- ○ **Reach for a toy she's dropped**
- ○ **Support her weight** when pulled to standing position
- ○ **Sleep about 14–16 hours per day**, several of which are during the daytime—sleep time is usually spaced out in two or three naps and a solid block of about six hours (sometimes much longer) at night

She's now ready for...

- ○ **A trip to a warm swimming pool** (by six months)—check to see if the pool has minimum age requirement for lessons
- ○ **A cup**, to experiment with and to learn the basics of sipping and drinking instead of just sucking
- ○ **A toothbrush**, and regular cleaning of her gums and emerging teeth
- ○ **Baby music** or movement classes, aimed at tiny tots
- ○ **Playtime with friends**—she'll be captivated by other babies and children, and probably want to get them into her mouth somehow, too
- ○ **A stroller that allows her to sit more upright**, to see the world around her
- ○ ....
- ○ ....
- ○ ....
- ○ ....
- ○ ....

Best toys and activities

Between three and six months your baby will discover how to use his hands, putting everything he can into his mouth. He'll also be developing a sense of humor, and will enjoy playing with you, laughing and smiling when you spend time together.

Best toys

- **Toys that don't have small parts that come off**, or strings or wires that could hurt your baby
- **Rattles are the perfect toy for this age**, and although your baby won't necessarily be able to control his movements, he'll love to make noise—choose one that fits neatly in his little hand
- **Baby gyms come into their own from three months**—choose one that reacts quickly to your baby's touch or kicks, allowing him to spin, grasp, push, pull, and manipulate the hanging objects
- **Squeaky, ringing, or crackling toys** respond easily to your baby's grip
- **Textured fabric toys** help your baby explore different sensations
- **Board books** with firm lift-the-flaps are excellent for reading together, and are also a good chunky toy for your baby to chew on or gaze at on his own
- **Blocks with "surprises"** will entertain your baby endlessly; as he examines them he'll be delighted by what's inside and the sound they make
- **Although he won't quite be ready for stacking toys**, rings that fit on to a central spike are a good idea, particularly if they are resilient enough for chewing, and easy for chubby hands to grasp
- **Stacking cups** make a satisfying noise when banged together, and your little one will enjoy swiping at towers and knocking them down
- **Bath toys** that squeak, leak, and float encourage your baby to bat at them and to learn to pour
- **A music box** that responds to your baby's touch with nursery rhymes or lively music will astound and amuse him when he learns that he can make things happen all by himself
- **Toys that pop up** when buttons are easily pressed will provide endless entertainment, and he will slowly become more adept at actually hitting the right spots to make the toys jump out

Playtime

- ○ **This is the perfect age to read** regularly to your baby; he will love sitting on your lap and listening to the sound of your voice as you point out colorful pictures, make animal sounds, and encourage him to lift flaps
- ○ **Try books with sounds and music that respond** when touched; they will help your baby learn that he can control things himself
- ○ **Place favorite toys just out of your baby's reach** to encourage him to move toward them—this will also help development of his balance, hand-eye coordination, and gross motor skills
- ○ **Provide plenty of things for your baby to kick**, including your hands; try to grab his feet as he lifts them, and see him laugh when he hits the target—make plenty of noise in response
- ○ **Prop your baby up on pillows** so that he has a view of his surroundings, this will also strengthen his neck and back
- ○ **Place your baby in front of a mirror**: he'll be fascinated by the "other baby," and will often smile at and talk to his new friend
- ○ **Encourage his cognitive development**, problem-solving ability, and memory by putting a ball under one of his toys or blankets, and encouraging him to find it
- ○ **Show him how to make things happen by himself** by banging a wooden spoon on a pot, for example
- ○ **Tickle, cuddle, and play with his arms and legs** as he gets used to new sensations and learns what his body can do
- ○ **Don't forget tummy time**, which will encourage a strong neck, excite his curiosity, and get him ready for crawling and rolling
- ○ ....
- ○ ....

Essential clothing and equipment

As your baby gets older, her needs will change slightly. You may find she's now ready for "real clothes" rather than just pajamas and onesies, and she may also be ready for more sophisticated equipment as her world increasingly extends beyond your lap.

To wear

- ○ **Your baby will still need regular changing**, so be practical and make sure that pants and other items are easy to put on and take off
- ○ **Avoid anything too complicated** that will irritate her skin or get in the way of her activities
- ○ **Snaps and well-padded zippers** are easier than buttons
- ○ **Make sure that any shirts and sweaters** have wide necks
- ○ **Everything should be machine washable**
- ○ **You might think about choosing a wardrobe in complementary colors**, so that leaks and spills don't mean a whole new outfit is needed
- ○ **Undershirts with snaps** under the crotch will keep your baby warm when shirts or dresses ride up
- ○ **Choose tops that also close over the crotch**, to avoid discomfort
- ○ **Make sure all of her clothing is loose and comfortable**, and that she isn't too hot—it's better to layer thin items than to give your child bulky, heavy clothing to wear
- ○ **Babies do not need shoes** until they are confidently walking, but you can keep little feet warm with booties or simple, soft-leather moccasin-type footwear; they may help keep her socks on, too
- ○ **If she constantly loses her socks**, why not consider a pair of tights—these are a good idea for boys, too
- ○ **Try to buy most of your socks in the same color**, so you don't face an endless pile of odd ones; however, there's nothing wrong with mismatched socks from time to time—just call it your baby's unique sense of style
- ○ **Make sure that your baby's outdoor wear has a good hood**—babies soon become adept at removing hats... and losing them

Equipment

- ◯ **Teething rings**—many babies start showing signs of teething around four months, so be prepared: avoid teethers that are made of PVC, and look for those that can be refrigerated to provide relief from discomfort
- ◯ **A chair**, which will allow her a wider view of her world, and perhaps allow her to bounce or swing when she moves her feet; something portable is best, so you can move baby from room to room
- ◯ **Bath toys**, which will hold her attention and make her look forward to sitting in the tub and getting clean
- ◯ **A sippy cup**—although she's not ready for solid foods yet, you can encourage her to start to drinking from a training cup
- ◯ **A baby toothbrush**—her teeth may not be emerging yet, but they'll be waiting under the surface, so it's a good idea to get into the habit of cleaning her gums before bedtime; you won't need toothpaste yet
- ◯ **A full-sized crib** (see page 55)—most little ones will have outgrown cradles and bassinets by this age, and now like to have more space to move around
- ◯ **An activity center**—these are safer than walkers and can keep your little one preoccupied with toys that spin, rattle, and light up while she gets used to standing, bouncing, and supporting her weight with her legs
- ◯ ______
- ◯ ______
- ◯ ______

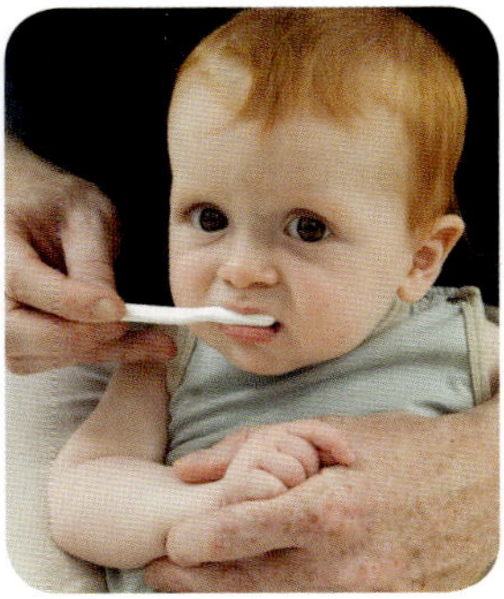

Is my baby ready for solid food?

You may find that your baby is hungrier than usual—but this doesn't necessarily mean that he's ready for solid food; you may just have to increase his formula intake, or allow him to nurse and feed more often.

Your baby is probably ready for solids if:

- ○ **He starts demanding feeds more often**, still seems hungry after his usual milk feed, and has stopped sleeping through the night
- ○ **He seems to show interest in what you are eating**
- ○ **He is able to sit up with support and control his head**
- ○ **He can move food around his mouth** when you feed him, or makes chewing motions even with no food in his mouth
- ○ **He can confidently put things into his mouth**
- ○ ....
- ○ ....

When to start

Health Canada, and the World Health Organization, have now stressed that weaning should not begin before six months (although a week or two earlier won't hurt); this will help minimize the risk of your baby developing adverse food reactions and allergies. Of course, each baby is different, and the exact timing will be decided by you and your baby's pediatrician.

Symptoms of food allergies

Although food allergies are uncommon in babies, they are on the increase, so if you have food allergies in your family on either side, it's a good idea to be aware of the symptoms before you begin introducing your baby to solid food. Contact your doctor if you're concerned.

Look out for:

- ○ **Vomiting or diarrhea**
- ○ **Gagging**
- ○ **Irritability**
- ○ **Severe colic**
- ○ **Eczema or skin rashes** (particularly around the mouth)
- ○ **Hives**
- ○ **Facial swelling**
- ○ **Breathing difficulties**

Symptoms can appear while your baby is feeding, or directly after, or within 48 hours. If breathing problems develop or his face swells, call an ambulance.

Food intolerance is slightly different, and doesn't involve your baby's immune system. Watch for symptoms suggesting that your baby can't tolerate certain foods well, since this can affect the nutrients he gets. Look out for:

- ○ **Chronic sniffling and excess mucus**
- ○ **Constipation or regular diarrhea**
- ○ **Eczema or skin rashes**
- ○ **Unusual fatigue**
- ○ **Constant indigestion or spitting up**
- ○ **Itchy eyes and skin**
- ○ **Sleep disturbance**
- ○ **Wheezing**
- ○ ______________________________
- ○ ______________________________

Teething

Your baby may not show any signs of teething or, indeed, teeth themselves, until well into her first year of life. Some babies, however, begin teething as early as three months, so it makes sense to be prepared.

Signs of teething

- ○ **Irritability and fussiness** as her gums become sore and painful; the first tooth is often the worst
- ○ **Drooling**
- ○ **Coughing or gagging**, as a result of extra saliva
- ○ **A rash on her chin**, mainly due to the drooling
- ○ **Gnawing, gumming, and biting everything** she puts in her mouth
- ○ **Rubbing her cheeks and pulling her ears**—the pain travels to the ear area and around the jaw
- ○ **Mild diarrhea**—this is a contentious one, since some professionals think this symptom is not linked, but a good Australian study recently found that slightly looser bowel movements are a common symptom
- ○ **A slightly raised temperature**—while a high fever is not a sign of teething and should be treated with caution, a low-grade fever can result from teething in some little ones; again, some doctors disagree, but parents report that it's very common
- ○ **Poor sleep**
- ○ **A runny nose**, as the ear, nose, and throat area become a little inflamed
- ○ ______
- ○ ______

It's all in the genes

The process of teething often follows hereditary patterns, so if you or your partner teethed early or late, your baby may follow the same pattern.

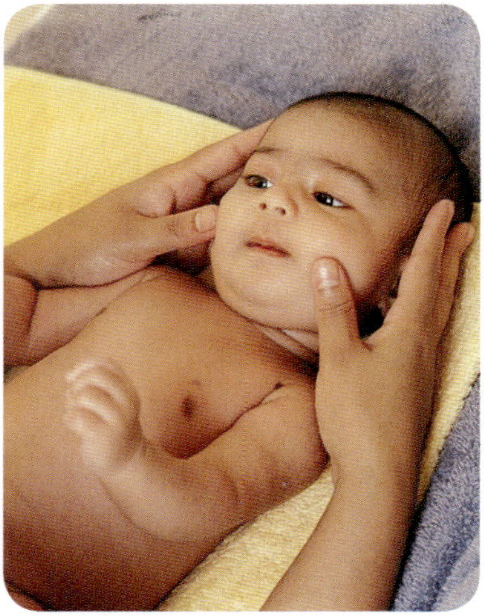

What to do

- ○ **Offer your baby a cool teething ring** (not one made of PVC) to gnaw on, and rub her gums with a clean finger
- ○ **Letting her chew on a clean, cool washcloth** may also help
- ○ **Look for a gentle teething gel** to rub into her gums—many contain benzocaine, a local anesthetic, so use sparingly; you may also consider giving acetaminophen for pain relief
- ○ **Homeopathic teething remedies** can be found in most large supermarkets and pharmacies, and usually contain the remedy Chamomilla, which is traditionally used to ease your baby's symptoms—check with your pediatrician before using
- ○ **If your baby has trouble sleeping**, gentle rocking may help
- ○ ....
- ○ ....
- ○ ....

Childhood illnesses

Even young babies can come into contact with childhood illnesses, and experience full-blown symptoms. It can help to be aware of what your baby could catch, and what to look out for. Breastfeeding moms who are immune will likely pass on their own immunity, and if your baby has been vaccinated, he will also have some immunity of his own.

Childhood illness	Incubation period	Symptoms
Measles	10 days	Fever, runny nose, cough, sore and reddened eyes, followed by a red-brown rash that usually starts on the face and spreads down the body about 3–7 days after the first symptoms appear
Mumps	2–3 weeks	Fever, headache, swelling of the main salivary glands producing a "chipmunk" appearance affecting the jaw, cheek, and neck
Rubella (German measles)	14–21 days	A light rash of pink dots, low-grade fever, aches and pains, headaches, sore throat, swelling of lymph nodes (glands) in the neck, loss of appetite
Whooping cough (pertussis)	About 7 days	Flu-like symptoms, runny nose, sneezing, low-grade fever, a cough that worsens over a couple of weeks and is worse at night, causing paroxysms that can make your baby's face turn blue or red; sometimes vomiting with coughing spells
Chicken pox	10–14 days	Headache, fever, general malaise, spots starting on the trunk and spreading to most parts of the body, appearing as little pimples that fill with fluid to form blisters that then crust over
Meningitis	Viral meningitis: 3–7 days Bacterial meningitis: 1–7 days	Viral meningitis tends to appear most often in summer months and is generally less severe; initially vague flu-like symptoms occur with fever and aches and pains, which develop over a couple of days. Bacterial meningitis is more severe, and symptoms can develop rapidly, often within hours. In babies and small children they include: stiff body with jerky movements (or extreme floppiness), irritability or dislike of being handled, shrill cry or unusual moaning, refusal to feed, tense or bulging fontanelle, pale blotchy skin, rapid breathing, fever. In older children look for a rash that doesn't fade under pressure (try pressing a glass against the skin)

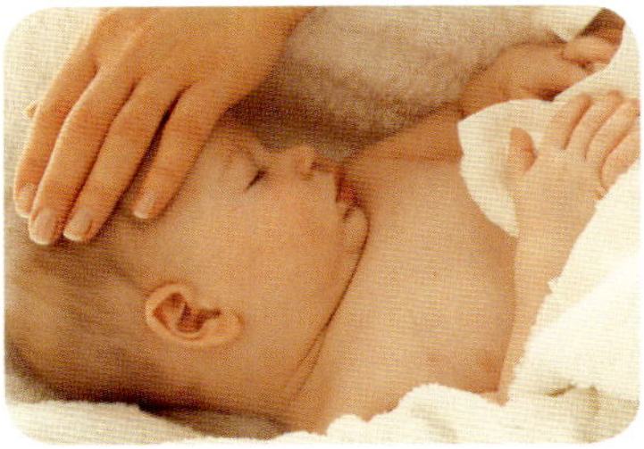

Boosting immunity

Although regular immunization means that most childhood illnesses are no longer prevalent, you should watch out for signs, and, if you are worried, contact your doctor.

	Treatment	Notes
	Painkillers and plenty of liquids; antibiotics for any secondary infection; plenty of fluids; keep your baby in a darkened room, since measles can cause sensitivity to bright light	
	Plenty of fluids, painkillers (acetaminophen), rest; use tepid water to sponge your baby down	
	Acetaminophen to bring down the fever; calamine lotion or mild corticosteroids to ease the rash; plenty of tepid baths	
	Antibiotics to clear the bacteria causing the infection; a vaporizer in the baby's environment; admission to the hospital is likely for babies under six months, to avoid complications like pneumonia	
	Calamine lotion to ease the itching; acetaminophen to reduce fever and discomfort; plenty of fluids; keep nails short and clean, or use mittens to prevent damage from scratching	
	If you suspect meningitis, you must seek emergency medical attention immediately—bacterial forms will require intravenous antibiotics; there is no treatment for viral meningitis, although medication may be offered to control the symptoms	

Your baby: 6–9 months

Developmental milestones

By the end of nine months, your baby will be a sociable, lively member of the family. You'll notice a dramatic change in her development as her coordination improves, and her little brain sets to work making sense of the world around her.

By nine months, your baby should:

- ◯ **Be eating solid food** along with her regular milk
- ◯ **Grasp objects** on her first or second try
- ◯ **See small objects easily**, and pick them up
- ◯ **Move a toy easily** from hand to hand, and sit and play with toys
- ◯ **Sit by herself** without pillows or other support
- ◯ **Enjoy standing** when you hold her up, and begin to pull herself up to stand at the furniture
- ◯ **Practice rolling** from her stomach to her back, and back again
- ◯ **Begin to crawl** on her hands and knees (some babies never crawl, but develop an efficient bottom-shuffle instead)
- ◯ **Move from lying down to sitting up**
- ◯ **Babble and make "b" sounds**
- ◯ **Enjoy blowing bubbles**
- ◯ **Turn her head when you call her name**
- ◯ **React positively when she sees you**—and perhaps laugh
- ◯ **Search for an item** that she sees you place out of sight
- ◯ **Explore everything with her mouth**
- ◯ **Show signs of picking up on your emotions**, perhaps smiling when you are happy, or frowning or looking worried when you sound or look angry
- ◯ **Start to imitate your actions**
- ◯ **Begin to reach out to you to be picked up**
- ◯ **Show the first signs of nervousness around strangers or separation anxiety** (see page 184)

She's now ready for ...

- ○ **Solid food**, and in increasing amounts—by nine months she should be eating three meals a day, and beginning to show less interest in her milk feedings
- ○ **A firm bedtime routine**, which she will now remember and anticipate
- ○ **Favorite books and bedtime stories**, which she will also remember and look forward to
- ○ **Saying her first word**—she may make a sound such as "ba" that she uses, with meaning, for many different things, followed shortly afterward by real words mixed in with the babble
- ○ ______________________
- ○ ______________________
- ○ ______________________
- ○ ______________________
- ○ ______________________

Best toys and activities

Your baby will be more mobile now, even if he hasn't yet developed the skills necessary to crawl. He'll enjoy the challenge of attempting to reach for toys and anything else that catches his interest, and his budding hand-eye coordination and motor-skill development mean that he'll become adept at playing with more sophisticated toys.

Best toys

- **Toys that encourage crawling**, tempting your baby to follow—buy toys on a string that you pull just out of his reach, or balls that he'll chase endlessly
- **Toys on a string** that he can pull toward him—but make sure the string is sturdy enough so it won't tangle or choke him
- **Toys that help your baby to explore different shapes and sounds**, as well as cause and effect, shape his thinking and motor skills—try stacking toys, shape-sorters, noisy blocks, and toys that ring, rattle, and crinkle
- **Activity boards** to help your baby to practice his coordination—he'll learn to open doors, twist, squeeze, shake, and pull things to get a reaction
- **Blocks that can be piled** and then knocked down are always popular
- **Containers that he can drop blocks into and then take them out**—watch him have fun with "dumping" games
- **A sturdy push toy** on which he can support his weight, pull himself up, and perhaps take a few unsteady steps

Playtime

- ○ **Your baby is becoming aware that objects still exist** even if he can't see them, so he'll love to play peekaboo and hide-and-seek games with a favorite toy
- ○ **Give him lots of objects to bang together**, and teach him how to play music with a pots-pans-and-wooden-spoon band
- ○ **Reading becomes more interactive at this age**, and he will enjoy touching the pictures, and even lifting some sturdy flaps; when you've finished reading, encourage him to turn the pages himself and "read" to you
- ○ **When you hear your baby babbling**, talk back to him
- ○ **Play simple fingers games**, such as "This little piggy" over and over and watch him delight as he anticipates the "wee wee wee all the way home"
- ○ **Because he is becoming better at remembering and anticipating**, any nursery rhymes or clapping games will excite him, as he looks forward to what comes next
- ○ **Encourage him to play on his own** (under supervision); doing so will help him become independent and more confident in his own abilities
- ○ **Lift your baby high in the air**, or bounce him on your legs; he'll love physical games, exercise, and motion
- ○ ....
- ○ ....
- ○ ....

A few toys at a time

Babies can easily become overwhelmed by a huge array of toys, so bring a few out of the toy box each day, and let your baby choose what he wants to play with. You can also put a small selection of toys in a box that he can reach into to choose what he wants.

Essential clothing and equipment

Your baby's clothing needs won't change much as she becomes more mobile, although you may wish to buy items with a little more padding to protect her knees and elbows. You will both, however, be ready for some new equipment as she forays into the world of solid food.

To wear

- ◯ **Loose-fitting clothing** that allows your baby to move easily is the order of the day, so make sure she's dressed comfortably
- ◯ **Three-quarter- or short-sleeved tops** will keep her hands free
- ◯ **Look for hard-wearing clothing**, particularly at the knees
- ◯ **Bibs are a definite necessity now**, and they should be either wipe-clean with a "tray" to collect food spills, or large and machine-washable
- ◯ **She'll need plenty of extra changes of clothing** as she begins to experiment with food; even the very best bibs can't protect her clothes from the mess she'll create
- ◯ **Consider a baby sleep sack**, which zips or fastens at the shoulders, to keep her warm in bed, since she's getting too big to swaddle
- ◯ **A pair of soft rubber booties** or an all-in-one fleece suit will allow her to remain dry and comfortable while she explores the outdoor world
- ◯ **Consider hats with under-chin fastenings**: removing and throwing hats is a popular baby game

Equipment

- ◯ **A jumper or a bouncing seat** that is suspended from a doorway—she may enjoy this as she becomes more confident and independent, and it will also give her legs a good workout
- ◯ **A toothbrush and toothpaste**—once she's eating, she'll need to have food debris cleared from her mouth twice a day, and when those teeth emerge they'll need to be brushed daily, too
- ◯ **A foldable "umbrella" stroller** is suitable from six months

- ○ **A sturdy high chair**—ensure it has an insert to snugly hold a younger baby; all high chairs should have a harness or five-point belt to prevent escapes
- ○ **A splash mat**, for under her chair
- ○ **2–3 small plastic bowls**, preferably with a suction cup to prevent her from firing the contents across the kitchen when you least expect it
- ○ **2–3 chunky plastic spoons** that her little hands can hold easily; she won't be able to feed herself yet, but you can encourage her to try
- ○ **2–3 weaning spoons**, with a small "scoop" to make her first attempts at feeding a little easier
- ○ **A plastic cup or a cup with a spout**; choose one with a "slow flow" so that she doesn't choke
- ○ ______________________________
- ○ ______________________________
- ○ ______________________________

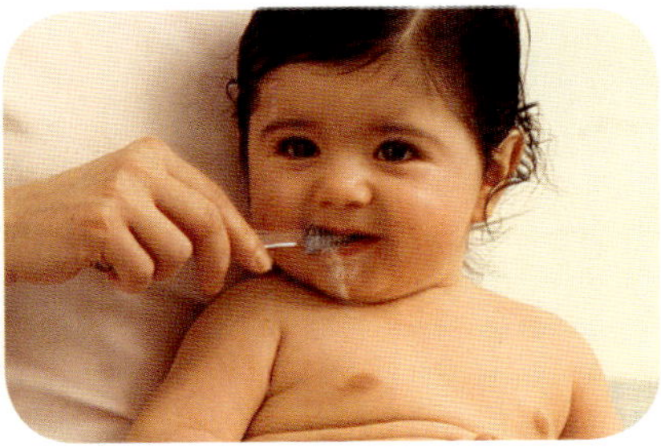

Equipment for preparing baby food

- ○ **A food processor** or hand-blender
- ○ **A hand-turned or electric grinder** (like you would use for coffee beans), which is ideal for potatoes, sweet potatoes, and other root vegetables that can become sticky and glutinous in a food processor
- ○ **An ice-cube tray** that is flexible so you can easily tip out your frozen purées; choose one with a secure lid
- ○ **Stick-on labels**: your purées will last for up to eight weeks in the freezer, and 24–48 hours in the fridge, so you may wish to label them with the date you made them and their contents
- ○ **Mini pots with lids**, to freeze larger quantities of your baby's favorites
- ○ ....
- ○ ....
- ○ ....

Tips for feeding solids

It's important to remember that for the first few weeks of weaning, your baby will rely on his milk for nutrition and hydration. First foods are designed to accustom your baby to different tastes and textures, and encourage him to develop the skills necessary to chew (or gum) foods and swallow them.

- ○ **First foods should be semi-liquid** and almost milk-like in consistency, to make them easy to swallow
- ○ **Add breastmilk**, formula, or a little cooled, boiled tap water to thin the purée if it's too thick
- ○ **Serve food at room temperature**, or just lukewarm—test a little on the inside of your wrist: you shouldn't feel it if it's the right temperature
- ○ **Thoroughly defrost frozen foods**, and then warm them with a little boiled water, or in the microwave—carefully stir anything you have microwaved, as it can contain hot spots
- ○ **Begin with some vegetables**, which aren't quite as sweet as fruit—little ones who begin with fruit tend to resist anything more savory, and can develop a sweet tooth
- ○ **Root vegetables are a good starter food**—try potatoes, carrots, sweet potatoes, and parsnips
- ○ **Strain fruit and vegetables with firmer skins**, such as berries or dried fruit, to ensure that they are smooth
- ○ **Once you've established some vegetables**, blend together fruit and vegetable purées before going on to the hard stuff: pure fruit purées
- ○ **Rice cereal is also good**, and can be used to thicken purées that are too watery—make sure your baby rice is smooth and creamy
- ○ **Encourage your baby to try some finger foods** (see page 164)
- ○ **Offer a new food every two or three days**, and watch carefully for any signs of a reaction (see page 145), particularly if your family has food allergies; note them in your foods diary (see page 162)
- ○ ....
- ○ ....

Best first foods and purées

Fruit and vegetable purées, along with rice cereal and other very finely ground grains, are ideal first foods. They will not only introduce your baby to different tastes and textures, but also give her a good boost of nutrients at the same time.

Start with one-fruit or one-vegetable purées, such as:

- ○ **Rice cereal**
- ○ **Avocado**
- ○ **Sweet potato**
- ○ **Potato**
- ○ **Carrot**
- ○ **Parsnip**
- ○ **Pumpkin**
- ○ **Apple**
- ○ **Pear**
- ○ **Banana**
- ○ **Apricot**
- ○ **Peach**
- ○ **Papaya**

Then try some blends:

- ○ **Root vegetables** (any blend you like)
- ○ **Carrot and squash**
- ○ **Broccoli and cauliflower**
- ○ **Lima beans and apple**
- ○ **Pea and pear**
- ○ **Lentil, celery, and carrot**

- ◯ Lentil and red pepper
- ◯ Spinach and potato
- ◯ Parsnip and potato
- ◯ Blueberry and melon
- ◯ Plum and pear
- ◯ Melon and mango
- ◯ Papaya and mango
- ◯ Peach and pear
- ◯ Banana and apricot
- ◯ Rice cereal and pear
- ◯ Strawberry and banana

And when she's got the hang of it...

- ◯ Chicken, spinach, and potato
- ◯ Codfish, potato, and carrots
- ◯ Chicken and sweet potato
- ◯ Turkey and broccoli
- ◯ Mango and strawberry
- ◯ ....
- ◯ ....
- ◯ ....
- ◯ ....
- ◯ ....

First foods diary

Jot down what your baby eats in the early days, and note any likes or dislikes, as well as any suspicious reactions, to form an invaluable record of her early eating habits, and make it easy to pinpoint any potential problems early on.

Food	Mixed with...	Date offered	Likes (yes/no)	Unusual reactions (immediate/within 48 hours)

Food	Mixed with...	Date offered	Likes (yes/no)	Unusual reactions (immediate/within 48 hours)

Great first finger foods

It's a good idea to offer finger foods alongside your baby's first purées, since they will help her to develop the skills she needs to feed herself. They'll also accustom her to different textures and tastes.

Try:

- ○ **Steamed vegetables**, such as carrots, broccoli, and cauliflower
- ○ **Graham crackers**
- ○ **Lightly toasted bread fingers**
- ○ **Melba toast**
- ○ **Miniature rice cakes**
- ○ **Very well-cooked pasta shapes**
- ○ **Chunks of tuna or poached chicken**
- ○ **Chunks of banana**
- ○ **Apple slices or chunks of mango or pear** (soft-cooked or canned)
- ○ **Peeled, sliced apricots**
- ○ **Peach slices**
- ○ **Soft blueberries**, halved and peeled
- ○ **Seedless grapes**, peeled and cut in quarters to prevent choking
- ○ ....
- ○ ....

Finger foods under supervision

Watch your baby carefully while she eats finger foods, since they can cause her to gag and choke. Encourage her to cough to expel the offending food. Try not to panic in her presence; you want your baby to associate mealtimes and food with pleasure and fun, not an anxious mom!

Ideal family meals

It's a good idea to get your baby accustomed to eating family food early on so she learns to enjoy the taste, and also feels part of the social experience of eating as a family. Be aware, however, that salt must not be added to food intended for babies under one year of age.

Suggestions for family meals that can be puréed:

- ◯ **Poached or steamed chicken with garden herbs** (anything goes), mashed potatoes, and green vegetables
- ◯ **Hearty root-vegetable soup**
- ◯ **Lightly steamed cod with spinach and new potatoes**
- ◯ **Meatballs in a light tomato sauce with noodles or rice**—if you grind the meat finely and make small meatballs, she can eat them as finger food
- ◯ **Sweet potato, carrot, and ginger soup**
- ◯ **Broccoli, leek, and cauliflower bake**
- ◯ **Dahl**—this Indian staple will introduce her to a number of fragrant spices, and is ideal for babies if you run it through the blender first
- ◯ **Fishcakes with avocado salad**—form her "cakes" into firm balls (make sure all of the bones are removed) before baking or lightly frying; her avocado can be puréed (skip the traditional squirt of lime—babies under one year should not eat citrus)
- ◯ **Shepherd's pie, with a creamy mashed-potato topping**
- ◯ **Fish pie with mashed-potato topping**
- ◯ **Oatmeal with fresh fruit purée** (give hers an extra spin in the blender and use her usual milk to thin)
- ◯ **Chicken and vegetable casserole**
- ◯ **Chicken poached with apricots, sweet potato, and grapes**, and served with rice for the family
- ◯ **Peach and apricot compôte**—serve yours with fresh yogurt, and hers with a little extra water as her own delicious dessert
- ◯ ....
- ◯ ....

Your baby: 9–12 months

Developmental milestones

Things are happening fast now, and you may find that you are rushing to keep up with your baby as she hones her crawling skills, and maneuvers herself around the house. Her curiosity is endless, and she now communicates with you in ways that you both understand.

By 12 months, your baby should:

- ○ **Confidently use a sippy cup**
- ○ **Be able to maneuver her spoon** to her mouth and have some success with her efforts at self-feeding
- ○ **Pick up toys and drop them for effect**
- ○ **Use her thumb and index finger** in a "pincer" grip to pick up small items
- ○ **Crawl confidently** forward and backward
- ○ **Pull herself up from the floor** to stand against the furniture, or you
- ○ **Cruise around the furniture**, supporting herself
- ○ **Indicate what she wants**—taking your hand if she wants a walk, or raising her arms if she wants to be held
- ○ **Point her finger to draw your attention to something** or show her interest
- ○ **Notice changes in your voice**—for example, firmness when you say "no" —and respond to them
- ○ **May understand the word "no,"** but probably not obey
- ○ **Recognize a few familiar words**, such as "bye-bye" or "milk"
- ○ **Recognize her name when she is called**
- ○ **Imitate you**—using her spoon, drinking from her cup, pretending to talk on her phone or waving good-bye
- ○ **Confidently put things in and out of containers**
- ○ **Show an interest in pictures and books**
- ○ **May use the words "mama" or "dada"** appropriately
- ○ **Cooperate in games**
- ○ **Play peekaboo or pat-a-cake**

She's now ready for...

- **Family meals**, which she will enjoy, and which will encourage her to eat a more varied diet
- **A new car seat**
- **Lots of outdoor play**, for example on the swings or in the sandpit
- **Food with more lumps** (finely chopped instead of puréed) and more exotic tastes
- **Conversations**—she will babble back when you talk to her and pause for her reply
- **A birthday party**... and opening presents
- ______
- ______
- ______
- ______
- ______

Best toys and activities

Being mobile changes your baby's world, and he will be into everything as he explores his surroundings. He'll be able to distinguish different objects, and will look for familiar toys.

Best toys

- **Toys that your baby can push around** the room are perfect now, and he will gain speed and dexterity as he heads toward his first birthday
- **Sorting toys, such as shape-sorters** and piles of big, chunky beads, will occupy your baby for hours
- **Balls** continue to be popular, and he will now travel in search of a ball when it rolls away, and even try throwing it himself
- **Sand tables** (or sandboxes) will provide endless enjoyment as he fills buckets, empties them, and makes a spectacular mess
- **Miniature versions of "adult toys,"** such as a chunky toy mobile phone, will appeal as babies begin to imitate their parents and caregivers
- **Interactive toys** hold new interest, and nothing will appeal to your baby more than pop-up toys and books that respond when he pushes a button
- **Wooden or sturdy plastic blocks** or containers are ideal, and by the end of his first year he should be able to stack a few of them confidently
- **Smaller objects to collect and a container to put them in** as he will be able to use a pincer grip effectively now
- **Basic, sturdy wooden puzzles with knobs** to lift the pieces in and out of position will appeal—choose very simple shapes at first

- **Toys with a string to pull**, since your baby can grasp and pull easily now—perhaps look for a toy that climbs up its string, or makes a sound or plays a song when its string is pulled
- **Any musical toys will appeal**, and bells, maracas, and even a drum will keep him busy and help improve his coordination and rhythm

Playtime

- **Let your baby explore and satisfy his curiosity**, opening cabinets, emptying drawers, and dumping out his toys from a basket
- **Help him build towers**, then knock them down
- **Fill plastic tubs and shoeboxes** with toys and let him examine them, and then empty and fill the tubs again
- **When your baby points to something**, name it for him—he'll love to know the names of familiar things and it will increase his vocabulary
- **Get down on the floor and chase him** when he begins to crawl
- **Choose books that he can interact with**, and "play" with the pictures (cover the cow's eyes, for example, or ask him to tickle the pig)
- **Teach him the sounds that animals make**, and see if he can imitate them
- **Singing and dancing** is a new trick you can try—clap your hands and sing favorite nursery rhymes, and encourage him to join in
- ....
- ....

Essential clothing and equipment

The day is approaching when your little one will be ready for her first pair of shoes, and her rapid growth means that a whole host of new clothes may be necessary. She may also have outgrown some of her baby equipment, and be ready for a bigger size.

To wear

- ○ **Her increasing mobility means that your baby will need sturdy, washable clothes** in darker-colored fabrics, to prevent endless piles of dirty laundry
- ○ **Choose clothing in complementary colors**, so that pieces can be easily mixed and matched and everything gets worn
- ○ **Your baby will show a new interest in being just like mom and dad**, and may like to have a pretty dress or a pair of jeans or socks just like yours
- ○ **She'll need three or four pairs of pajamas without feet**—she'll enjoy using her bare feet to help her keep her balance
- ○ **A warm, waterproof winter jacket** is a must now, as she will escape the confines of her stroller as often as she can and needs that extra warmth
- ○ **If you live in a cold climate** and winter has hit, choose mittens that attach to her coat with a plastic clip
- ○ **One or two pairs of rugged pants**, such as jeans, and some comfortable sweatpants are ideal for a growing, increasingly mobile baby, no matter what the sex
- ○ **Warm-up pants and wide-necked, slip-on tops** (avoid buttons and ties—your baby won't hold still long enough to get them fastened)
- ○ **Non-slip socks** will help to give your baby some traction as she attempts to maneuver herself to her feet, or slide across the floor; let her go barefoot, too, when it's warm enough

Time to take on the stairs

Even with safety gates, your baby needs to learn how to use the stairs. Teach her to crawl up, then slide back down on her bottom, holding onto the railing.

Equipment

- ○ **Safety equipment is essential now**—make sure you have locks on all cupboards and drawers with contents that may not be safe; you may even need a fridge lock if your little one is inquisitive
- ○ **Invest in a good safety gate** at the top and bottom of all stairs with more than three steps
- ○ **Look carefully around your house and baby-proof** everything with the appropriate equipment (see page 115)
- ○ **Now that she's standing**, you'll want to lower the base of her crib so she can't climb or fall out
- ○ **She'll be ready for her own safe, chunky utensils**, and will enjoy copying mom and dad by using a fork and spoon
- ○ **A backpack-style carrier** may now make it easier to carry baby, as she grows too heavy to be carried at the front
- ○ **Your baby will probably be ready to graduate to the next-stage car seat** at around nine months; check the label to be sure she hasn't already outgrown the one she has
- ○ ....
- ○ ....

Your baby's first birthday

Your baby's first birthday is a momentous event, and you may wish to celebrate with a small party. Don't be surprised, though, if he doesn't show much interest in the proceedings, or if he finds the paper and the packaging more exciting than his birthday presents.

- **Keep it simple**—you can't enjoy celebrating your baby's transition to toddlerhood if you are busy serving hors d'ouevres
- **Limit the number of guests**—most babies suffer from separation and stranger anxiety at this stage (see page 184), and a big gathering may cause distress rather than enjoyment
- **Keep things short**—an hour or 90 minutes is probably the full extent of his attention span
- **Set the time for the party half an hour after he normally wakes up from his nap**, so he's refreshed and not too grumpy
- **Forget about themes and party games**—your baby will have no interest, and you may end up feeling deflated

A select few

Invite only a handful of family or friends that your baby knows well, so as not to overwhelm him on his first birthday.

- ○ **Entertainment for little ones** can be cheap and simple—a pot of bubbles will keep them entranced for ages
- ○ **Balloons may be fun**, but place them out of reach to avoid him popping them, or choking when they are deflated; better still, choose helium balloons and cut the strings so the little ones can't reach them
- ○ **Make sure he's had something to eat and drink** before the guests arrive; even the most baby-friendly food probably won't appeal to him in the midst of all the excitement
- ○ **Let him open his presents**—this will be the highlight of his day, if only because he will be surrounded by a mountain of crinkly, colorful paper
- ○ **You may choose to do party favors for older guests**, but a shiny new ball will be enough to enthral his one-year-old buddies when they leave
- ○ **Watch the sugar**—most little ones haven't had much experience, and can become sick and irritable on a party-food diet
- ○ **You can make an exception to the rule** by making a wonderful, wobbly Jell-O, perhaps moulded in the shape of your baby's favorite animal
- ○ **By all means make him a cake** in the shape of something he recognizes—a farm animal, for example, or perhaps a teddy bear
- ○ **Offer water to drink** (most baby guests will have their own cups), and some fun, healthy finger foods (see page 164)
- ○ **If anyone asks for gift ideas, suggest books**—this is the best way to build up your baby's library, and it's an affordable gift for most people
- ○ **If grandparents want to be more generous**, perhaps you could suggest they buy your baby his first ride-on toy, which will probably occupy him for the rest of the day
- ○ **Don't forget your camera**—this is one day you can't fail to record
- ○ **Take a photo of all the guests**, and tape it in your baby's scrapbook; you'll be amazed how quickly you forget his first friends, as he grows up and develops his own social circle
- ○ ....
- ○ ....
- ○ ....

Going back to work

Preparing for your return to work

Even the most hardened career woman can't fail to feel a wrench when first leaving her baby to return to work, and circumstances may mean that you have to return earlier than you'd like. Here are some tips to help you get ready for going back to work and for coping with the first few weeks as a working mom.

- ○ **Going back to work doesn't mean you have to give up breastfeeding**—investigate whether you can have access to a quiet place to pump and a fridge for storing your milk while you are at work
- ○ **Start pumping in the weeks before you return**, and fill up your freezer—frozen breastmilk will last several months in a sealed container
- ○ **Make sure you've got your childcare lined up** well in advance (see pages 181–183) and that you've had several trial sessions—if your baby is used to her new routine, she won't crumble when you leave for your first day back
- ○ **Make contact with your boss and colleagues** a week or two before your official return date, to touch base and catch up on what has been going on in your absence—you'll feel more confident if you are prepared
- ○ **Bring your baby in to work a few weeks before your return**, during the lunch hour, perhaps—you'll remind colleagues of why you've been away, and give them a chance to soften when they see your beautiful baby
- ○ **Consider starting back at work on a Wednesday or Thursday**, so that you don't have a whole week to get through as soon as you are back
- ○ **Once you are back, try to stick to your schedule**; unfortunately, some people resent women who have had time off work to have a baby, and may be looking for opportunities to prove that you can't juggle both
- ○ **Try to compartmentalize**—plan a regular phone call to your child's caregiver to check on things and make sure you are reachable in case of emergency, then buckle down and focus on your work
- ○ **Finally, take care of yourself**—juggling a baby, a household, and a job can be exhausting, so make sure you take regular breaks, drink plenty of water throughout the day, and eat well
- ○ ....
- ○ ....

Working alternatives

Working part- or flex-time can be the ideal solution for women who want or need to work, but who also want to spend more time with their babies in the early years. Another option is, of course, working from home. In all cases, you do need to be focused on work in the hours you've agreed, and self-disciplined enough to ensure that you achieve everything your job entails within the appropriate hours. It's all too easy to get bogged down in home and/or work life, and everyone suffers as a result. Define your hours clearly, and make sure you are doing the job of mom when you are with your baby, and career woman when you are at work.

Survival tips for working moms

It's not easy to get the balance between home and work life right, even at the best of times, and throwing a baby into the equation can make things downright difficult. There are, however, plenty of ways to ensure that you don't just survive, but thrive!

- ○ **Don't try to be superwoman**—you can't be perfect at everything, and if the housework slides, your baby doesn't get his bath one night, or you turn on a DVD instead of stimulating your baby, the world won't end
- ○ **Treat your child's caregiver(s) with respect**—you need her, and you need her to be happy when she is looking after your precious baby
- ○ **Learn to say no**—put your baby, your family, and your job at the top of the list of your priorities, and then work out what else makes sense and enhances your life; say no to anyone or anything that you don't enjoy
- ○ **Don't feel guilty**—many working women would choose not to work, but if that isn't an option, embrace your situation and do the best you can
- ○ **Take care of yourself**—an exhausted, underfed, and emotionally strung-out mom isn't any good to anyone; you'll be capable of keeping more balls in the air if you look after yourself
- ○ **Take care of your relationships**—your partner or husband is part of the team, too, and needs lots of love, time, and respect
- ○ **Always have a plan B**—things have a habit of not going according to plan, and if you always have a contingency in place, life is a lot easier
- ○ **Establish clear guidelines at work**—you may once have been a 24-hour-a-day employee, but that is no longer possible; if everyone knows where you stand at the outset, resentment is less likely to breed
- ○ **Find some support in other working moms**—they can be a fountain of great ideas for coping with daily challenges and occasional crises; they'll also be an invaluable support network when the going gets tough
- ○ **Job-share at home**—make sure you divvy up the chores and the childcare, so that both you and your partner get the break you need
- ○ ....
- ○ ....

How to choose a day-care center

Places at good day-care centers get booked up very quickly, and it can take some time to find the right one for you and for your baby's needs. Start looking into facilities that might be suitable as soon as you know you are going to return to work—if possible, during your pregnancy.

Look for:

- **A high staff-to-child ratio**—there are laws about the number of little ones that can be cared for by each responsible adult
- **Separate spaces for younger and older children**, meaning your baby gets the care he needs without the distractions of older kids
- **A strong, fair discipline policy** that matches your own beliefs
- **Permanent staff members** with good first-aid skills, as well as experience dealing with childhood illnesses and providing medical attention
- **Well-trained staff** who constantly update their knowledge, and understand child nutrition, development, and common issues
- **Warm, friendly, and loving staff**, who clearly show interest in the children
- **A designated staff member** to be your main contact
- **A sound policy and clear evidence of safety and security**
- **Plenty of age-related opportunities for your baby to be stimulated**
- **A good selection of clean, tidy toys, and age-appropriate books**
- **A quiet place for little ones to sleep**, and a clean place for them to be fed
- **A policy of informing parents on their babies' progress daily**
- **A good open-door policy**, so that you feel you are welcome at any time
- **A provincial or territorial licence**, a glowing inspection report by the relevant provincial authority, a public health and fire department certificate, and several good personal references: ask around—other parents won't lie
- **Above all, trust your instincts**—if you see contented babies and warm, caring staff, you are probably on to a good thing
-
-

How to choose a nanny

It is daunting to hand over your baby to someone else to look after. You will need to develop a close relationship with your child's caregiver, so take the time to interview prospective nannies well in advance, then go with your gut feelings: they are almost always right.

- **Draw up a full job description**, involving every aspect of your baby's day-to-day care, and what you'd like to see happening
- **Write this down in a bullet-pointed list**, so you can talk through each aspect and issue and get feedback, ideas, and opinions
- **Make sure you have your baby in tow at interviews**—prospective nannies should be interested, playful, and affectionate with her
- **Check that she has emergency first-aid training** and ask to see her childcare certifications, diplomas, and driver's licence
- **Talk to at least two personal and professional references**
- **Her basic knowledge of and views on child development** should be up to date and consistent with yours
- **She should have plenty of ideas for stimulating your baby**
- **She should share your approach to nutrition and meal planning**, or be prepared to adopt it
- **She should absolutely share your views on discipline**
- **Organizational skills are essential**, and she should be able to keep track of everything in your little one's daily life
- **Ask where she sees herself in five years' time**—continuity of care is important to small children
- **Ask for details of her strengths and weaknesses**, and be wary if she says she has none of the latter
- **Make sure she's flexible**, and won't mind working longer hours from time to time, or planning some of her holidays when you have yours

How to choose a home day care

Having your baby looked after in someone else's home is often a good solution to the childcare dilemma, and your little one will benefit from the company of a small group of other children. Look for:

- ○ **Not too many children**—there are laws outlining how many children of each age can be cared for, and it's important that this is maintained
- ○ **A cheerful, friendly demeanor**, and an obvious interest n children
- ○ **Someone with plenty of ideas**, willingly outlined, for stimulating your baby and keeping tabs on her development
- ○ **A clean, welcoming, smoke-free home**, with an outdoor play area
- ○ **Knowledge and experience of first aid**
- ○ **A similar approach to yours to discipline, potty training, nutrition, and TV viewing**
- ○ **A willingness to enter into a contract** that outlines hours, sick pay, what happens when your child is ill, changes to your child's routine, and payment
- ○ **Flexibility**, so if you are running late or have an early start, you are covered
- ○ **Some provinces license home-based caregivers** and inspect them—you should check to see if there is a report you can view; also check for a registration certificate, if applicable, and references from other parents
- ○ ....
- ○ ....

Keeping track

Ask your caregiver to write down some notes each day about what your baby did, including what she ate, what she played with, when she slept and for how long, and any milestones she may have reached.

Soothing separation anxiety

Separation anxiety normally rears its head at about six months of age, when your baby has developed a strong attachment to you as his primary caregiver. There are, however, plenty of ways to ease the pain of separation, and make the experience more positive for you both.

- **Don't go out of your way to avoid separations** when your baby is young—he should get used to being with other people
- **You can try to leave the room** for a couple of seconds at a time, and then reappear—this will help him learn from a young age that you will always return after you go away

Be kind to yourself

Bear in mind that guilt is a destructive emotion, and can undermine your self-confidence and even your relationship with your baby. All moms suffer from "bad-mother syndrome" from time to time. Accept that this is par for the course, and then make a conscious effort to pat yourself on the back for managing to juggle so many areas of your life. You are doing the best you can and most likely you are doing a wonderful job, so make sure you acknowledge that, and believe in the fact that both you and your baby are capable of being happy and fulfilled with a working-mom lifestyle.

- ◯ **Introduce new babysitters (and childcare settings) gradually**, letting your baby get to know them before being left alone with them
- ◯ **Provide transitional objects**, such as a favorite teddy or blanket, which your baby will use to cope with separation; leaving behind a scarf or shirt with your scent firmly embedded can also help to ease the transition
- ◯ **Try not to make light of your baby's distress**—comfort him and reassure him; tell him that you know he is sad and that you love him and will be back soon
- ◯ **Always say good-bye**—disappearing will make your baby feel insecure; if you say good-bye, he'll soon understand that this means you are leaving and he'll also start to remember that you always come back
- ◯ **Don't be surprised if your baby needs lots of reassurance** before and after separations—spend some time offering just that
- ◯ **Show plenty of warmth and approval for your caregiver**—if your baby knows you are comfortable with her, he will feel happier in her care
- ◯ **Talk it up**—show pleasure and excitement that you are going to the day care, or that your nanny is about to arrive; if you are positive about the experience, your baby will pick up the right signals and soon follow suit
- ◯ **Similarly, try not to cry or appear anxious**—if he senses something is wrong, your baby may become even more distressed; you have to go to work, and he will have a wonderful, fulfilling time while you are gone
- ◯ **Try as much as possible to return on time**—if you don't turn up when your baby expects you to (in time to bathe him, for example, or to give him a nighttime feeding), he may become anxious and distrustful
- ◯ **Remember that you can suffer from separation anxiety, too**—reassure yourself that you have chosen a good, reliable caregiver that you trust, and that your baby will be safe and happy with her
- ◯ ....
- ◯ ....
- ◯ ....

Covering vacations and illness

Even the most carefully set up childcare arrangements can fall to pieces from time to time, when your baby or your caregiver is ill, or your nanny takes a vacation. It's a good idea to have contingency plans set up in advance for emergencies, and to help get you through periods when no one is available to hold the baby.

- **All children get sick**, and babies and very young children are particularly susceptible because of their immature immune systems—make sure you are aware of any sickness policies at your day-care center
- **Remember that all caregivers are entitled to vacation** (and vacation pay), so it's a good idea to establish at the outset when they might take place
- **Check with your employer** to establish what their policy is about taking time off when your children are ill, so you know what to expect—you may be required to use up your personal sick days
- **You might be able to arrange to work at home** when your child is ill—it's a good idea to establish remote access with your work computer, and to have some work ready that you can do from home if you can't get into the office
- **Working at home is a good option for longer periods of illness**, or for times when your nanny is off; perhaps a babysitter or "mother's helper" can work for you for part of the day to help make sure you get work done
- **You may be entitled to personal emergency leave**, which allows you a certain amount of unpaid time off—but be prepared: just because it's law doesn't mean that your employers and colleagues will like it
- **See if you can take turns with your partner to care for your child**
- **Ask another mom in advance** if she would be prepared to share her nanny or au pair to help you out in a pinch—you could offer the same in return, or something similar, such as an evening's babysitting
- **Establish a strong support network** at work and with any other moms at your child's childcare facility—it's easier to arrange swaps and ask for favors if you are on a first-name basis
- **Try not to feel guilty about asking for favors**; we are all conditioned to think that asking for help is a sign of weakness, but working moms need all the help they can get
- **Set up a roster of family members or friends** who can help at short notice

- **Be honest with your work colleagues**—they'll appreciate the fact that you are up-front about your position, and probably be only too glad to help out
- **Check out babysitter agencies in advance**—you will have to pay for having help at short notice, but it can save you a lot of hassle and concern
- **Plan for your nanny's vacations or day-care closings in advance** by arranging short-term cover—a local high-school or college student might be only too glad to earn some extra money helping out
- **Consider arranging your own vacations** when your caregiver is taking a break; you'll remove the pressure of finding help, and you'll enjoy the experience of sharing time as a family
- ......
- ......
- ......
- ......

Staying at home

Staying at home with your baby may seem like a luxury to some, but it may well be the hardest job you'll ever do. However, every ounce of patience spent and every nerve frayed will result in the most rewarding experience of your life.

- ○ **It goes without saying that it should be financially feasible**—if staying at home is going to send you into massive debt and put enormous pressure on your family relationships, you may need to rethink
- ○ **Try living on one salary** for a couple of months before or just after your baby is born, putting any maternity pay you receive in a savings account—if you can manage, then give it a try
- ○ **Consider the benefits you may lose, too**—if you depend on your employer for pension or other retirement savings plan contributions, healthcare benefits, or a company car, there might be more of a financial hole than salary numbers alone suggest
- ○ **Find out which benefits your partner can get through his job**—it might be more cost-effective for your partner to stay at home with the baby
- ○ **Make sure you establish a good network of other moms with babies**—not only is the stimulation important for you both, but you'll be party to a wealth of shared ideas, concerns, and wisdom
- ○ **Make sure your partner appreciates your efforts** and takes some responsibility for the household chores, too; don't feel you have to be superwoman—your priority is your baby's health and well-being
- ○ **Take time out to read the paper** and to get the housework and shopping done—little ones do need to grow up understanding that there are other things that require mom's or dad's attention from time to time
- ○ **Keep up with courses or activities that will keep your work skills sharp**, so that if you do go back to work you'll be ready
- ○ ....
- ○ ....
- ○ ....

Index

Useful websites

Pregnancy and birth

- www.babycenter.ca
  www.caringforkids.cps.ca (Canadian Pediatric Society)
  www.sogc.org (Society of Obstetricians and Gynaecologists of Canada)
  www.phac-aspc.gc.ca/hp-gs/index-eng.php (Public Health Agency of Canada's Healthy Pregnancy site)
  www.motherisk.org (Information on the safety of medications, infections, chemicals, personal products and everyday exposures during pregnancy and breastfeeding)
  www.canadianparents.ca

Childbirth

- www.canadianmidwives.org
  www.doulacare.ca
  www.lamaze.org
  www.multiplebirthscanada.org
  www.sweethomebirth.com

Breastfeeding advice

- www.lllc.ca (La Leche League Canada)
  www.canadianbreastfeedingfoundation.org

Maternity Rights and Benefits

- www.servicecanada.gc.ca/eng/ei/types/special.shtml#Who (EI and Maternity and Parental Benefits information)
  www.rqap.gouv.qc.ca/index_en.asp (Quebec Parental Insurance Plan information)

Childcare benefits

- www.cra-arc.gc.ca/uccb (Universal Child Care Benefit)
  www.cra-arc.gc.ca/bnfts/cctb/menu-eng.html (Canada Child Tax Benefit)

Child Development

- www.growinghealthykids.com
  www.childdevelopmentinfo.com

Acknowledgments

Author's Acknowledgments

The author would like to thank Peggy Vance, Penny Warren, and Helen Murray at DK for coming up with a great idea, and pushing to make sure it happened. Thanks to Angela Baynham and Helen for excellent editing and ideas, and Hannah Moore and Liz Sephton for a lovely design. I'm also grateful to the National Childbirth Trust, Annabel Karmel, and AIMS for information, as well as to homeopath and hynotherapist Melanie Woollcombe. New moms Karol Allen and Erica Manger made sure I got it right, and have tried and tested the checklists for accuracy. Finally, thanks to my own little one, Marcus, and the older two, Cole and Luke, who gave me the experience I needed to write this book.

Publisher's Acknowledgments

DK would like to thank Hilary Bird for the index, Salima Hirani for proofreading, and Lizzie Ette for checking the information in the book.

Picture Credits

The publisher would like to thank the following for their kind permission to reproduce their photographs:

Corbis: image100 71 (left); Mother & Baby Picture Library: Ian Hooton 112 (left)

For further information see:
www.dkimages.com